From the Bottle
to
the Bible

© Stanley Nolt, 2018

All rights reserved. No part of this book may be reproduced or transmitted in any form or by any means, electronic or mechanical, including photocopying, recording, or by any information storage or retrieval system, without permission in writing from the copyright holders.

Written with Shawn Smucker
Edited by Gina Gumby
Cover Design by Josh Loudenslager

To my Lord and Savior
Jesus Christ
who made me a new man.

Table of Contents

Chapter One: Easy Money…1

Chapter Two: In the Beginning…3

Chapter Three: The Life of an Alcoholic…14

Chapter Four: Flying by the Seat of My Pants…27

Chapter Five: Running South…42

Chapter Six: Turning Bad Money into Good…61

Chapter Seven: Returning to Church…72

Chapter Eight: Life After Addiction…86

Chapter Nine: Going Back to the Bars…106

Chapter Ten: A Home for the Broken…121

Chapter Eleven: The Spirit World is Real…143

Chapter Twelve: Freedom…151

CHAPTER ONE
EASY MONEY

    I sat in the dark, holding my gun, leaning back against a tree in this small wooded area in the middle of a wealthy, gated community. There were no street lights, and the stars were bright through the branches. Occasionally a lone car would cruise down the neighboring road, and I'd sit up straighter, wait to see where it was going. But no one stopped at the house.

    After a few minutes, I stood up and walked as quietly as I could through the undergrowth to a spot where I could see the other side of the house. Then I crouched down and waited. The only lights on in the house came through the basement windows. Everything else was dark. Another car drove past. I stood and walked back to my first spot.

I didn't even know exactly what I was on the lookout for. I guess I was making sure no one else showed up, or that the African guys didn't leave with the money. I was pretty jacked up in the moment, adrenaline pumping. I had taken nearly a million dollars from inside the walls of the truck, a million dollars that wasn't mine, and put it up as collateral in this scheme. If we lost that money, the real owners of it wouldn't let us survive. I knew that much.

Could the guys working with us contact someone from outside? Could they lead them to my house and take everything? I didn't know. It was simply a matter of making sure no one showed up. That was the only thing I cared about.

I thought a lot about my life that night. I thought a lot about the events in my life that had led me to that moment. There was something that saddened me about the entire situation. I knew we could make a boatload of cash if this whole thing worked out well, but even the thought of that left me feeling empty.

It was 3am. I crept through the woods and back to my car. I thought I'd go back to my motel and crash for a few hours before coming back to the house and seeing how the operation was going. It looked like everything was going according to plan.

Little did I know, it wasn't.

CHAPTER TWO
IN THE BEGINNING

It was a blazing hot summer day in 1983, and I was 16 years old. I was a big kid for my age, sturdy and strong. I was also a hard worker, and eager to earn my way in the world. I had always been a bit of a trouble maker, but at 16 I could finally head out on my own. I guess you could say I was trying to find my way.

A friend had connected me with a farmer up in Akron, PA, a big-time guy with half a dozen farms and a ton of land. I think most of his farms, those days, were focused on tobacco production. Anyway, he took me on and once he saw how hard I worked, kept me busy. I worked long days that summer for him, usually out in the fields.

Tobacco is a hands-on kind of crop, and it

requires a lot of work. You plant the young tobacco plants by hand, in long rows. You harvest them the same way, one at a time, slicing off the stalks, spearing them with a long lathe that gets heavier and heavier as you go along. Farmers like tobacco because it's a cash crop, something that brings them in some much-needed money in the late winter. But it's hard work.

On this particular day it was late summer, around noon, when the air just feels heavy. I was sweating like crazy, and I stood up for a moment and looked out over the field. The guy I worked with wasn't far away, bent over a tobacco plant. He stood up and wiped sweat from his forehead, looked over at me. We nodded at each other, then went back to work. Once we harvested the tobacco stalks, they'd be hung to dry in a barn. Then, the dried leaves would be placed in sizer boxes and sold.

I was a Mennonite kid in those days, with my parents raising me in the Mennonite church. I grew up on a farm, too, but ours was a chicken farm, and we had barns full of layers. I was used to hard work. I was used to sweating for a day's wages. Being out there in that field felt like home.

During the hottest part of the day, we stopped to take a break. The wife of the guy I worked with came out into the field, dragging a cooler behind her. I don't remember if she met him every day, but on that day she brought some drinks out. We were a little way apart, me and the other guy, and he called me over, so I put down my tobacco spear and stretched, then walked towards him, carefully stepping over and between the large plants we hadn't yet harvested.

"Hey, kid," he said with a smile on his face. "You want a beer?"

I peeked into the cooler and there they sat, those cold drinks lost in the ice. They were dark brown bottles, and beads of sweat already dripped down off them. The ice made a clinking sound as he reached in, grabbed one by the neck, and held it out to me.

"You want one?" he asked again.

I had never had a beer in my life. The Mennonite community I grew up in was very conservative, and anything like alcohol was forbidden. No movies, no television, no dancing, no radio – the list went on. It wasn't that we talked about it much; you just knew the rules, and drinking alcohol was definitely against the rules.

But it was hot. And I was thirsty. And those bottles of beer looked nice and cold. So I reached out and took one.

"Yeah," I said, shrugging. "Sure."

Why not? No one from my family or church

was there. This guy didn't care if I drank or not. So I lifted it to my lips and drank it down. That cold drink cooled me off and filled me right up. Before I knew it, I had put down three of them. We sat there in the dirt and talked for a little while before standing, stretching, and going back to work cutting off the tobacco stalks and lining them on the spear all the way down the row, backs bent over, and all the way back up.

In that moment, when I drank that beer, something changed inside me. It was like a switch got flipped, a switch I never even knew existed. My body got a craving for alcohol that could not be filled, a desire that would not go away for decades. I craved beer from there on out. It's hard to explain how something I had never encountered before could have such a sudden, fierce hold on me, but it did.

I was hot and sweating and those three beers barely gave me a buzz. We charged through our work that day, right through the heat. I don't know if I felt guilty about drinking those bottles of beer or not. I went home that night and didn't think too much about it. But I knew I wanted more.

Less than a week later I went to work on another farm owned by the same farmer, a place back in Wernersville. I happened to be working with the same fellow whose wife had brought the cooler of beer into the field. It was another long, hard day of work. I always enjoyed that feeling I got at the end of a day like that. We finished a little early that afternoon, so on the way home we stopped at a bar and had some drinks.

I felt another rush of excitement, walking into the dark bar and sitting down on the stool beside my co-worker. I had never done anything like that before. It was a new, exhilarating experience. I ordered a beer, and no one said a word.

How could a 16-year-old get served? you might wonder. When I was in the 2nd grade, I looked like a 5th grader. By the time I was 16, I looked like I was in my 20s. I was always big for my age, and in those days (as long as I wasn't with my friends), I could walk into just about any bar and get served without any fuss. Plus, in the early 80s these places really didn't card you as much as they do today.

Anyway, there I sat, 16 years old, drinking a significant amount of beer for the second time in a week. The alcohol had its hooks in me. I had no idea at the time just how deep those hooks would go.

My parents were good parents, good people. My dad drove a truck, not long haul, but we still didn't see him much, since his schedule usually had him leaving around 4am and getting home around 11pm.

We had two chicken houses there on the farm, built when I was around five or six years old. That was my life growing up: church, school, and working the farm. I had a good mom. She was around when dad was not, and she kept things orderly, kept us all moving in the right direction.

I was one of seven kids, second to the oldest (there were five brothers and two sisters), and that farm provided good work for us boys – we always had something to do. Our house was a busy place, and there was no such thing as being bored. Because of my early years, I really don't know how to live without working. It's in my bones.

Looking back on my childhood now, even before I started drinking, I feel like I was always getting into trouble. I just never really felt like I fit in with the other kids. I was always doing things the teacher didn't approve of. And in my private Mennonite school, I became the scapegoat, blamed whenever something was broken or went wrong, whether or not I was at fault. Granted, I often was, but when you're always being blamed for stuff, at some point you decide you might as well be the one making all the trouble. The feedback you get at an early age can shape the way you think of yourself. It became part of who I was, "the bad kid," and I was all too happy to play the role.

I wonder if I had some kind of a learning disability, like Attention Deficit Disorder. As I think back on those early years, I realize that much of my trouble stemmed from an inability to focus, an inability to concentrate on what the teacher was talking about. I always forgot what she said, even right after she said it. Words and numbers on the chalkboard went all fuzzy inside my head. When I hit that wall, I'd give up.

Of course, then I'd get in trouble. The teacher would keep me inside for recess. I'd get mad that I couldn't go out, and I'd break something or say something, or do something. It was a never-ending cycle of making the wrong choice, being harshly disciplined, and then acting out in revenge.

Bad went to worse.

One night, the director of the school board came to my parents' house to have a discussion about my behavior in school. I guess my behavior had reached a point where they felt something more had to be done about it. My brothers and I had these little battery-powered walkie-talkies, so I took a popsicle stick and taped it against the button so that it would stay on. I hid the walkie-talkie under the sofa because I wanted to hear what they were saying about me.

I listened to the entire meeting, and I didn't like what I was hearing. I felt so wronged; much of what the director said seemed harsh to me, like they were looking for the bad in me, instead of looking for the good. Some of the things he blamed me for were things I hadn't even done. Even though I misbehaved, I had a very deep sense of justice, and when I felt like people were treating me (or others) unfairly, it made me very angry.

I ran out of the house to the barn and grabbed my BB gun. It was dark outside by then. I pumped my BB gun and aimed it at the director's car, and shot a hole in the back window. As would often happen, as soon as I acted out, I regretted it. I ran back into the house and stayed in my room.

The director didn't even realize what had happened at first, because it was dark, but as he drove home, I guess the crack spread and the window fell into the car. He called my parents. My brothers told my dad what had happened, what I had done. It was just another episode in my storied childhood.

But it was also kind of a turning point. That was in the 6th grade, and I got expelled for an entire week of school, right in the middle of the year. At the end of the year I was told I wasn't welcome to come back. My mother switched us all to a different school, and within six months I was in the same trouble at the new school. I was drawn to the troublemakers, and I couldn't break out of the rut I found myself in.

But in my heart of hearts, I knew I wasn't a bad kid. My mom has often said, since then, that of all the kids, I had perhaps the softest heart. When she was sick, she'd tell me to go out and play, but before she knew it I'd be back in, beside her bed, asking if there was anything I could do for her, asking if she was okay. I cared deeply for the people I loved.

There was certainly a battle going on inside of me, battling forces between good and evil. I was pulled back and forth between the two. This is, unfortunately, a battle that would rage for many years to come.

My father was a very outgoing man who all the neighbors liked, but he had a very short fuse. If you did something wrong, before you knew it, wham! You found out about it. Both of my parents were very set in their old Mennonite ways. They still are. We attended the Horning Church in the Weaverland Conference.

I don't mean to make it sound miserable – all in all, I had a good childhood. My parents were good to us. One time, we went to Niagara Falls for vacation, and I was amazed at that incredible sight. Once a year or so we'd go to a cabin as a family, and those times are ingrained in my mind as overwhelmingly good, incredibly fun. But for the most part we stayed home – we had the seven-acre farm to look after, and of course there was always the chickens. And whenever we returned from any of those trips, my own troubles resurfaced.

It also seemed like we were gathering eggs nonstop. I guess we kind of were. We had 45,000 chickens, all of them in cages, and we had to gather their eggs every morning and every evening. Maybe around 40,000 eggs every day. The eggs, collected automatically, came along belts to one end of the chicken house, and then there was the main belt that brought the eggs across the front of the chicken house, gliding all of those eggs into the packing room. We kids would pack the eggs onto flats, store them in the cooler, and trucks would take the eggs off to buyers every couple of days. I guess we worked around 2 ½ hours in the morning and the same in the evening, packaging eggs.

We were busy, and life was busy, and the years passed us by. There were no major events that led me deeper into trouble, and there were certainly no moments where I suddenly became the perfect kid. Life went on.

But that day in the field when my co-worker gave me those bottles of beer, the day I had my first taste of alcohol, as I look back on my life, that feels like a turning point to me. It was certainly the beginning of my downward trek into alcoholism. There was something about alcohol that kept pulling me back. Something in that alcohol had latched onto my mind and wouldn't let go.

I was an alcoholic from that first drink.

CHAPTER THREE
THE LIFE OF AN ALCOHOLIC

My church friends didn't follow me down that road, and for the most part, they didn't get into trouble with me. I had one friend who drank with me. As we got older, a group of us started taking trips up to a cabin in the woods. I always took a few six-packs with me – I didn't sit there getting drunk all weekend, but I certainly felt the need to have alcohol along. Even in those early days, I wouldn't think of going a weekend without drinking.

My buddies' reactions were mixed. A few of them got upset with me and came down kind of hard, saying I shouldn't have brought it along. A few laughed about it and thought it was kind of funny. Some didn't care one way or the other. Only one guy drank with me.

I think my parents, without talking to me about it, decided they were going to become more proactive in changing my life for the better. They had certainly tried everything else though the years: discipline, taking away privileges, even changing schools. When that didn't work, I guess they thought a change in scenery and responsibility might do the trick.

So, when I was 19 years old, my dad bought a second farm up in Rahrersburg, PA, and it kind of became my responsibility to run it. I moved onto that farm, and he built a hog barn on the property. I took care of things for him, living my own life at a relatively young age. It was a lot of work, and I can't say I enjoyed it. I think maybe it was something my dad did to try and tame me down. Maybe he thought more work would bring me back into line. And I guess it worked for a little while, but I didn't like taking care of pigs. In fact, it got to the point where I hated it, and I wasn't very good at it.

I got married when I was 21 years old and my wife and I lived there on the farm for a short time. I looked around for something different to do. I started doing a little truck driving on the side when I was 19 or 20 years old, still living on my dad's hog farm and taking care of that, but I had time to do some local deliveries. I started getting busier with that, and eventually I told my dad the farm thing wasn't working out for me. In total, I was there for seven years, about five while I was married, but the memories I have of that time are foggy.

One thing that sticks out to me from those years is that I was always part of the fire company. I had joined one in Schoeneck when I was fifteen years old, and then when I moved up to Rehrersburg I joined the one up there. For a couple of years, I was the chief engineer and even became the assistant chief for many years. I enjoyed hanging out with the guys and helping people. After I got married, it became a place for me to go off to and have some alone time.

It was also where I did most of my drinking. There was a social quarters there at the fire station, and I stopped in almost every night. All of those years, I don't think my wife really knew how much I was drinking. At least not in the early days. I guess she probably picked up on it a little bit here and there, but I don't think she had any idea how serious a problem it had become for me. By the time she did, it was too late.

It wasn't like I hid it from her or tried all that hard to keep it a secret. I just separated those worlds, my home life from my drinking life. I drank at the fire station and at the local bars, and I tried to keep everything else in its proper place.

My drinking was very much like how smoking

becomes for some people, the way people crave a cigarette. I needed it every day. If I'm honest with myself, I have to admit that it started causing problems for me early on. Drinking drew me away from my family, and it limited how successful I could become at truck driving.

Of course, I never would have owned up to that when it was happening, but I think drinking alcohol is why my farming years didn't go so well.

My dad sold the pig farm and I started truck driving full time. One thing led to another and my truck driving turned into me owning a small garage where I'd work on other people's trucks. Then it became a full-time truck repair shop. Soon, I was doing service calls in the middle of the night, taking a wrecker out and picking up truck drivers who got stranded in the middle of the night. It was good money, and soon I knew just about everything about trucks you could know.

The late-night service trips also often turned into pit stops at the local bars. Honestly, my drinking just overtook my desire for anything else. It wasn't that I stopped working – I was an aggressive, hard worker. All my life I worked. But to continue to manage a business, to function on a day-to-day basis with that much alcohol constantly in my system, well, I'm not sure how I got by. Drinking took first place.

I opened a truck shop at the intersection of Interstate 78 and Route 419, in Bethel, somewhere around 1996. Bethel was four miles away from where my wife and I lived. It became my life, that garage. I became an expert on repairing trucks, pricing trucks, and buying broken down trucks. I spent hours there, working on trucks and talking to drivers. I threw myself into this new business with everything I had.

You know, throughout my life I was mostly happy. I was never someone who struggled with depression or anxiety. But all my life I was also searching for something, never satisfied with what I had. I always thought there must be more to life – there must be something else out there somewhere that would make things a little bit better. I'd start something, and then six months later I wanted to do something different. Always. I never really stuck to one thing, not my entire life.

There was always something out there on the horizon. Something else. But when I got there, when I finally arrived at that new thing, my satisfaction only lasted a short time before I saw another horizon and chased that one down. I was always running after something.

I'd say my wife and I had a good marriage in the early days. We were both happy then. But I was never satisfied with church. I went there because every Sunday morning, well, we went to church. It simply was. There was no other life, no other way to spend a Sunday morning. The Horning Church service usually lasted about two hours, and there was no Sunday evening or Wednesday evening church, so I sort of tolerated it, but I wasn't satisfied there. For my wife, though, that was her church. Her father was a bishop there, and she was very dedicated. She still is. So was the rest of my family.

The divide between us continued to widen as I spent more of my time working on trucks, and more of my time drinking. The church interested me less and less.

Of course, it wasn't all doom and gloom. As I look back, the poor decisions I made tend to overshadow that time of my life, but there were good times, too. We traveled a lot with the kids in those early days. We bought a motorhome and went up to the cabin. There was a lot of happiness in those days. The only negative things that happened were things I brought into the picture with me, my obsession with the business, my drinking and all the things that came with that. I think we could have had a very happy life. It's amazing to me how alcohol can wind its way in and poison every aspect of your life.

I remember one especially late night, around midnight, and I was sitting back in a bar room, drinking down some beer. It was probably around 1999 or thereabouts. My trucking business was cruising along, and I even had a few employees working for me. I'm not sure why I was out that night. Maybe someone had called for a tow and afterwards I decided to make a quick pit stop at the bar. I certainly did that from time to time.

Anyway, a bunch of my friends were at the bar and I kept drinking. Turns out though, one of my truck drivers was in another state somewhere, broken down and trying to reach me. When he couldn't get ahold of me, he tried my house and spoke with my wife. So then my wife went out looking for me. I guess the fact that she knew where I was will tell you a little bit about how much she knew at the time. I guess she probably knew more about what I was up to than she let on.

She came walking into that bar room and she pulled me out. I think my friends just sat there in shockthat she would come looking for me, that she would come into the bar, and that she would have the gumption to drag me out.

It's sad for me to talk about. I knew in those

days that my drinking was breaking her heart. I knew it was hurting her and the rest of the family. But I felt powerless to stop. Besides, why should I stop? I had no reason to stop. In my mind, everything was fine, and anyone who voiced concerns over my drinking just didn't know what they were talking about. I was fine.

But not that night. That night everything didn't feel fine. Seeing my wife coming into that bar, having her find me like that, in that environment, was a terrible thing.

She got me to my truck in the parking lot without a word, and then she walked out to her car and left. I was stunned. Shocked. I made up my mind that night that I was finished drinking. I got into my truck (completely drunk) and drove over to my truck garage. I was intending to get my broken down truck sorted out, but right across from the truck garage was a church. I couldn't drive by it without stopping. Something made me pull my truck into that church parking lot.

I parked and sat there in my truck, thinking about my life and where I had gotten myself. I remembered my first drink in the middle of that hot summer field. I thought about my wife and kids. It felt like my life was falling apart and I had no power to stop it. I was so drunk I got out of the truck and just threw up over and over again. I called my wife from the parking lot of that church. I was feeling heavy with the weight of all the different ways I had let her down.

"Do you want me to come home or should I just leave?" I asked her. I felt like I was at rock bottom. I still remember what she told me.

"No," she said. "Please come home."

Please come home.

So I did. First I went back to my truck garage and dealt with the broken-down truck situation. Then I went home. I slept on the sofa that night, got up a few times in the dark to throw up. I spent a lot of time in the bathroom that night, and during all those trips back and forth from the sofa to the toilet, I told myself I was finished.

I was done. I wouldn't live that life anymore.

And you know what?

I quit.

I quit drinking, quit smoking, quit everything. This was in 1999 or thereabouts. I went four or five months without drinking or smoking, and life was normal, and I was sober. I had a dream during that time, and in my dream I was taking people with addictions to a mission in New York City. I remember waking up and feeling so hopeful.

You would think this was the beginning of something good. And for those four or five months, that's how it felt. Maybe my life was changing. Maybe I could do this on my own. Maybe all of that drinking was just a time in my life I would one day look back on.

But after a little while, I started drinking again. It always started with one little drink. Once a week. Then twice a week. Before I knew it, I'd be back to drinking every day, then every chance I had. Before I knew it, I'd be stopping in at the bars late at night again.

Every time I decided I was going to quit, I ended up going back. I entered this cycle of quitting and drinking again, quitting and drinking again, and each time I dove back into the drinking world it got worse. Consistently, it got worse. I drank more and more after each dry period. I fell deeper and deeper into it.

These were such sad times for my family. These are hard times for me to think back on.

At some point during those days, my sons planned to go to New York to do some deer hunting, my oldest son was around 17 years old. They were going to meet up there with my wife's brother, and they stopped at Cabella's to buy an extra box of bullets to take along. But they weren't old enough to purchase the ammunition, and the store wouldn't sell it to them.

So they called me to see if I could meet them there to buy those bullets. Of course, I was in a bar drinking at the time, but I dropped everything and drove up there to meet them and buy those bullets for them. They didn't say anything when I saw them, but I'm sure they had to smell the alcohol on my breath.

I bought the ammunition and after I left they drove up to New York to go hunting. Meanwhile, I drove myself back to the bar, and when I got there and sat down and I cried. It hit me like a ton of bricks. I wished I was going with them. And if I would have been in my right mind, if I wouldn't have been drinking, I would have done that. I would have gone along. I should have gone along.

That's one of the memories that really sticks with me, and it still hurts. It's crazy what alcohol will do to you.

Another time I walked out of the bar just as my wife's Suburban drove past, and they were out spotting deer. They just so happened to drive by the bar I was at. It was like a punch to the gut, that reminder of what I was missing out on.

We were all missing each other, I guess, though I could see the solution right there in front of me: walk away from alcohol. I just didn't have the strength to do it.

My wife took the kids up to a cabin for a

weekend with one of her sisters. My youngest daughter, six or seven years old at the time, said she wanted to go a certain way to the cabin, out the interstate. So they went that way, and one of her sisters asked her why she wanted to take that particular road.

"I wanted to go past the junk yard to see if I could see my dad before we go," she said.

When I heard that later, well, it had a profound effect on me. But I was so bound up in my addiction, and it was such a stronghold in my life, that even heart-wrenching stories like that couldn't change me. It affected me, but it wasn't enough to break the chains of addiction in my life.

The crazy thing is, I never had a DUI, never had an accident, and never got arrested for it. I had drivers on the road, but I drove, too, occasionally. You might think that since my job involved driving, that was motivation to quit. But it was the opposite. Being on the road all the time meant I was away from home. I could do whatever I wanted to do.

For quite a while my trucking company hauled dedicated loads out of Wisconsin. We hauled farm equipment from there back to Pennsylvania, New York, and New Jersey. So I'd find a random load to take out to Milwaukee or Green Bay, unload in the afternoon, and then drive over to the farming equipment factory in the afternoon. I wanted to be the first one to load up in the morning in order to hit the road early, so I stayed close.

About eight miles from the factory was a Holiday Inn that had a bar. I'd always park up there and drink all night. Sometimes those were lonely nights at a quiet bar, just me and my thoughts. On other nights some of the factory workers I got to know would meet me over there. They were a fun-loving bunch, and we'd sit there long into the night.

There was many a night I'd leave there at midnight and drive to the factory in my tractor trailer, so drunk I couldn't even see the yellow line on the road. But at daybreak I was right there at the loading dock, the first one to get loaded up and head out. I felt great in the morning. The cool air cleared my head and life always seemed hopeful in the morning, like things would get better. I could almost believe it on those mornings when I was driving east into the sunrise. I could almost believe my life would get better.

I drove all the way home, and I'd arrive at my destination that night or early the next morning to unload. I was always functioning. A functioning alcoholic. But as the years went by, I drank more and more. My thirst for it increased.

CHAPTER FOUR
FLYING BY THE SEAT OF MY PANTS

I remember that night very clearly. It was a kind of measuring point, a stone in the road that marked how far I had fallen. I was hanging out at a local bar when some of my friends got out some cocaine. I was used to that. My drinking friends were always doing drugs. I was around it all the time. But it was never a temptation for me. Not even a little bit. I was quite content to spend my days in the haze alcohol produced. I didn't need to get high.

"You're crazy," I often said in a serious voice, shaking my head. "What do you do that for? That's nuts – it's going to kill you one of these days."

One night, late at night, I was sitting there in the bar with a few of my friends, and we were on a long, slow binge of alcohol. The lights were dim and I was killing time. I had nowhere to go. I had been there for hours. A guy I occasionally drank with needed a ride home, and he lived just over the Blue Mountain in Schuylkill County.

"I can give you a ride home," I said, not thinking much of it. It was late, but I didn't want to go home, and I didn't feel like sleeping in the truck garage again, at least not yet. So he climbed into my car and we hit the road.

I was completely wasted, driving drunk. That's when this guy in the passenger seat reached in to his pocket and pulled out a small plastic package of cocaine. He grabbed some kind of a book from the glove compartment of my car and laid the cocaine on there in straight, white lines. He took his time, and I really didn't care. What he did with his money and his time was his own business. He turned a little map light on, an interior light, and I could see it there on the book, the cocaine. Two little white lines.

"You just snort it up your nose," he said. "Easy as pie."

He took a straw and sucked one of the lines up his nose. He shook his head and cleared his throat. He sniffed a few times to clear his nose. Then he looked over and held the book with its one remaining white line in front of me, over the steering wheel.

I wish I could say I took some time to think about what I was doing, but for some reason all of my defenses were down that night. I didn't even hesitate. After so many years of not doing drugs, in one instant I gave in. I snorted that cocaine while I was driving down the road and it hit me hard.

We went to his house and I dropped him off, at first planning on heading back to the truck garage where I'd spend the night. But on second thought, I went inside. He lived in the basement of his parents' house in a two-story building. He had a little apartment in there, and it was a nice place. Well put together. Clean. It wasn't like a drug den, something you'd find in the city. He wasn't a low-life – his parents were middle class people and they lived in a nice area. I followed him in.

A couple more people showed up in the wee hours of the morning, and I snorted enough cocaine that night to kill an elephant. The dam had burst, and I jumped into drugs with the same enthusiasm I had taken to alcohol. In fact, the same thing happened. The same exact thing as when I took that first drink in the field on that hot summer day. It was just a different demon, one I snorted inside of me.

That was the beginning of the end for me.

That's when my life spiraled completely out of control. I was so high that night, and I was drinking alcohol on top of it. It was like I had completely given up on everything, thrown in the towel.

My emotional life was a wreck, numbed by alcohol and now drugs. My family life was nonexistent. I spent more and more evenings sleeping at my shop, never making it home. Days were a haze of work and recovering from the night before and pushing for that next thing, and nights blurred together, full of drugs and alcohol.

Somehow, I kept my business going. It even thrived. Occasionally I would tow a tractor trailer that was totaled, so I started buying salvage trucks and selling the parts. I could make good money because I knew how to repair engines. I knew which parts were worth the most, and I could then sell the refurbished engines for a hefty profit. I parked the trucks I bought in the grassy areas around my shop.

The township wasn't too happy about that – I guess they thought it was an eyesore, having all those trucks parked around the garage. Technically, I wasn't allowed to park huge tractor trailers on my property because I didn't have the right permits. After a few letters from the township, I sold everything, cleaned up the property, and complied with their request.

But a few months later I stumbled on to some good deals, bought a few more trucks, and the whole thing started again. A year later the township stopped me again. After running through this scenario three or four times, they sent a certified letter and threatened to fine me. By then I was doing pretty well fixing up totaled trucks and refurbishing engines, so I started looking around for some space to keep the trucks I was buying.

In 2006, I ended up renting a salvage yard at the Midway exit on Route 78, in Bethel, PA. The guy who owned it before me kept cars on the lot, but when I moved in he sold all of the cars and made space for me to park the wrecked trucks I bought. I was able to spread out and take that business to the next level, and, as I did with everything else, I jumped in full bore.

So I was selling parts and getting into that business. He also had a towing business that he operated out of that salvage yard, and I bought that from him in 2007. I had an office there and a small apartment, too. It was a nice little efficiency, and it worked out well for me because a lot of the work I did was night work.

I started staying at the apartment at the new property in Bethel on nights when I got too drunk.

Even then, I just couldn't stand seeing how my drinking and doing drugs was hurting my family. It killed me to see them so upset. I started spending more and more nights there at the salvage yard apartment. Then weekends. Soon I was basically living there, and we were separated, though we never had a conversation about it. Everything just kind of happened.

This is how drugs and alcohol work – slowly they dig in their claws, and at first it hurts, but after some time passes, the pain numbs. You drink and drug more to numb whatever you do feel. Soon, you don't feel anything. And you'll do whatever you can to keep it that way.

When I took over this guy's towing business, I had a contract with the state police. I did all of the inspections on their cars, changed the oil, changed out the tires, that sort of thing. I picked up a contract with the local township cops as well. There were police officers coming through my garage and salvage yard every day, all the time. I was always working on their cars, and they started calling me when there was an accident that involved a car that needed to be towed in the middle of the night. I started to recognize and know some of the cops by name. They were nice guys, and they appreciated my availability to help them out. We had a good working relationship.

The business grew and grew, and it was all by word of mouth. I never advertised or anything. I think my location right there off the highway helped, too. My salvage business started to attract the attention of some overseas folks looking for engines and truck parts, and I filled shipping containers for them to ship stuff all around the world.

When you're in the salvage business, and you stick to your word, and when people realize you're reliable, then they want to keep working with you. A guy from Jamaica started coming in on a regular basis, looking around, buying parts and sending them overseas. He was a nice guy, very laid back, and we sort of hit it off. One day he came to buy some truck parts and I guess he noticed I was high. If he noticed it, then surely the police officers who came through noticed it, too, but if they did, they never said anything about it.

"Hey, Stan," he said in a kind voice. "You know, there's a reason I am sending all of these truck parts overseas."

I listened.

"I'm actually bringing marijuana up from Jamaica, and I'm paying for it with truck parts that I send back down there."

The parts were his currency. That was how he

laundered his drug money. It made sense. I had heard of people doing that within the salvage industry. It was always a business that was full of corruption and illegal activity.

He paused, waiting to see how I would respond. I shrugged my shoulders. To be honest, it didn't bother me, what he did with the parts. It wasn't any of my business.

"You want to get in on the action?" he asked me, raising his eyebrows.

Well, I didn't see that coming.

I didn't have to think about it for too long. I was always itching to try new things, especially if it involved making money. For some reason, whether or not it was legal never bothered me. Maybe that was a remnant of my bad-boy status from when I was a kid. I don't know. But I shrugged my shoulders and laughed.

"Why not?" I said to him.

I continued helping him ship his truck parts to Jamaica, but I also started buying bales of marijuana from him to resell locally. When he was in the area, I'd meet him in a neighboring city and pick up bales that were compressed and shrink-wrapped, rectangular bales of green, dried leaves. I didn't really think too much of it. It was just the next thing on the horizon, and I thought I'd be able to make some good money reselling it.

I was so careless with my drug operation that I sometimes wonder if I wanted to get caught. I'd meet up with him, pay him cash, and then take those 15- to 30-pound bales of marijuana and just throw them in the back of my truck like a hay bale and drive home. I never covered them, even though my salvage yard was constantly crawling with cops. I never took many precautions.

Once I had the bale in the house, I had to unwrap it from the plastic and then break it apart. The marijuana leaves were very dry and so tightly shrink-wrapped that I had to use a hammer and a chisel to get it all apart, and once I finally had all of the marijuana broken up and ready for bagging, it was around a three-foot high pile sitting there on the floor in my living room.

I went and got a small scale and worked my way through the pile, weighing it out into one-pound plastic baggies. Then I'd sell the one-pound bags to local dealers, the guys on the streets who were reselling it to the user. I'd start off by giving them a free bag, and I'd meet up with them the next week, collect the money they made selling the first bag, and give them another one to go out and sell. I drove a motorcycle in those days, and I'd pack the saddlebags full of these zip-lock baggies of marijuana, then go out and make my runs through the towns in the area.

I never felt nervous or afraid. Nothing scared me in those days. I never thought I'd get caught, not even when I was sitting in my apartment, bagging marijuana, looking out the window and watching the state police walk around in my truck yard waiting for their cars to be ready. There was a park bench there in the front, and they'd sit there, enjoying the sunshine, waiting for their cars. Or they'd be in the office, hanging out, and just a few doors down from my apartment while I measured out a 3-foot high pile of marijuana. I think they knew I was involved in stuff, but they had no clue to the extent of it.

I had a great working relationship with the police. Sometimes they'd call, especially the township cops, when they themselves were drunk at a bar somewhere and needed a ride. They knew they could count on me to pick them up in the middle of the night and not say a word about it. Sometimes I'd go pick up the police car with the tow truck and give them a ride to wherever their own car was parked.

Other times, they'd be out doing a DUI bust and they'd call me to come get the car of the person they were arresting. Well, I'd show up to tow the car to the impound lot and I was more drunk than the guy getting busted for the DUI! But I knew so much about most of them, and had some dirt on a few of them. I knew what they were up to, so when it came to me and the stuff I was into, they just looked the other way. It became a whole situation of them scratching my back if I scratched theirs.

Why did I sell marijuana? I guess I did it for the money. It was something else to do, some other potential pot of gold at the end of the rainbow. I mean, I had the potential to make a lot of money doing that. I got the bales from the Jamaican at a very good price, and there was a high margin but I tended to smoke away a lot of my profits.

Eventually, though, I was making enough money selling drugs (marijuana and cocaine by that point) that I kind of ignored the towing business. It followed the same pattern as all of my other ideas: I built it up, really focused on it, made something of it, and when it wasn't fun anymore, I passed it on to someone else to take care of.

I hired a guy to run the towing business for me. Not too long after that, I got a letter from the state police headquarters. Someone was on to me. They cut me off. There was a date for the end of the contract, and it was a week later. They weren't doing business with me anymore – no towing, no inspections, nothing.

I always knew the main guy there wanted to stop using my garage, but he didn't have the nerve to end it on his own, so he relied on the state headquarters to get in touch with me. No one wanted to be the bad guy.

The police gave me the majority of my business, so that was basically the end of my towing business. I sold off the tow trucks, keeping only one or two of them to have around for my salvage business. But things generally continued more or less the same. I worked. I drank. I did drugs. I kept living my life in the same old haze, always looking for that next challenge, that next distraction.

My relationship with my parents at that time was basically nonexistent. I didn't even go to their house on the holidays. My mom called every so often, always checking in on me, always wondering when I was going to move home with my wife and kids. Always wondering when I'd return to the church. She had good intentions, and I know she loved me, but there wasn't anything anyone could say at that point to change me. I was too far gone. The only one who could change me at that point was God himself.

But my parents, my family, they got frustrated because they couldn't do anything for me. I was doing what I wanted to do, living my own life. I still respected them; it wasn't like I trashed them or talked bad about them, but I had gone my own way. For the most part they left me alone.

A few people from the Mennonite church would stop in at the salvage yard occasionally to talk to me. I knew why they were there. They wanted to convert me, to bring me back into the fold. But when they showed up, I knew how to talk as if everything was fine and good, and I steered the conversation away from what they wanted to talk about, away from me and my problems. I knew how to play the game.

The fact is, my friends and family had no idea how deep into it I was. They had no idea.

For three or four years solid, I was never sober. I woke up in the morning and drank beer for breakfast. I was always drinking. That's what I did. That's all I did. Keeping alcohol in my system was the basics of life. I didn't even think about it anymore.

Selling marijuana led to me selling pretty much any drug you can imagine. I got connected with higher ups who dealt in large amounts of cocaine and heroin, and I started selling that, too. Then I started using all of it. From around 2007 to 2010, all through those years, I can't remember ever being sober.

Around 2008 or 2009 I filed for divorce, but my

wife wouldn't sign the papers. She didn't believe in divorce, and she refused to give up. That languished for a while, and eventually I backed away from trying to get a divorce. I just let it go. The papers sat there on my counter, and it got close to when the judge could have signed them without my wife's signature, but for some reason I never pursued it. Eventually I threw it all in the trash. I didn't want to think about it anymore.

Every so often I tried to reach out to her. For what exactly, I don't know. But she had family around who protected her from me. And I understand that. I wasn't exactly the kind of guy you'd want your daughter or sister living with. I don't know if that's even what I wanted or why I tried to reach out to her. I was in a haze. We never made a connection.

The only thing I know I wanted in those days was to live a carefree life. That's it. I veered away from anything that looked like responsibility, anything that looked like commitment. I wanted to be able to do whatever I wanted to do, on any given day, without having to think too much about it. I thought that was freedom, and I tried to center my life around that.

This meant that everything I did, I did haphazardly. I was a bootlegger in everything I did. I drove a truck for three or four years without a CDL license. I just drove. I didn't care, and I couldn't be bothered to go through the hassle of getting the right license. I'd go through DOT checks. I'd even get pulled over. No one ever caught it. No one ever saw it. I can't explain it. Sometimes I'd go a year without a current IFTA. I had stickers, but my IFTA had actually expired because I didn't file my quarterlies the way I was supposed to. I flew by the seat of my pants in everything I did. Everything. All I wanted was a carefree life.

The reason I did so well in my businesses, my towing business and my salvage yard, my trucking business, and my truck repair shop, was because I knew trucks better than anyone. People came from all over the country to have me work on their trucks. I knew what I was doing. I could always figure things out. There was never a problem I couldn't diagnose.

But even though I was good at what I did, that didn't mean I was good at running a business. The paperwork, the office part, it was terrible. Terrible. I'd get inspection licenses to inspect vehicles and a year later I'd get revoked because I didn't turn in my paperwork. Stupid stuff like that, I did it all the time. To this day I hate anything having to do with paperwork.

I was flying by the seat of my pants. It really was only a matter of time before everything came crashing down around me.

CHAPTER FIVE
RUNNING SOUTH

January 3rd, 2008. I remember that New Year's week well. I was at a point in my life where I couldn't stand being around anyone. I wouldn't say that I hated people, but if it was up to me, I'd spend every day and night on my own, alone. Talking to people tired me out, and it seemed like it was always the same old thing, over and over again. Everything was so empty.

My family had disappeared from my life, which was my fault. I never saw my wife and kids anymore and rarely saw my parents. I had no one in my life anymore besides my drinking and drugging buddies, and that whole scene was tiring me out.

But I didn't see any way out of it. My life, the way I lived it, the things I was addicted to, had become everything. There was nothing to my life besides waking up, drinking beer, doing drugs, and going back to sleep. Sprinkled in there somewhere was work and the businesses I ran, but I couldn't have cared less about them.

I wanted to be alone. I wanted to be by myself without anyone talking my ear off or bringing up their problems. I didn't want to deal with customers or business or paperwork. I didn't even want the hassle of dealing drugs. I just wanted to be on my own. That's when I had an idea.

I owned a small boat that I kept down in Maryland on the Chesapeake Bay, a motorboat that I enjoyed taking out onto the water and getting away from things. It was January 3rd, the middle of winter. It was cold. But the boat called me, so I drove down and got on board. It didn't take long to get the boat ready. Soon everything was in order, and I was heading south.

Being out there on my own wasn't the smartest thing to do, but it felt great. I started heading down through the bay out of Northeast, MD. I was alone, and that's what I had been looking for. Those winter waves were short and choppy. The sea was rough, and it was 25 degrees outside. I didn't realize it, but the boat pounding in the waves was causing a lot of spray, and the spray was freezing immediately when it hit the boat.

My windows started icing up.

But I never had second thoughts about heading out. I was desperate to get away, so even though I didn't know where I was going or what I was doing, I kept sailing. I had it in my head that I was going to go south, just keep sailing south. That was all I knew.

The layer of ice on the boat kept getting thicker, so I pulled into a marina and tied up after sailing for about four hours. It can be dangerous when your boat gets covered over in ice – it can make the boat top heavy, and if it gets bad enough it could even tip over in the water. That's the main danger.

I stayed in that spot for two days, and the weather cleared up and the sun came out. The ice melted off the boat, and I worked my way south to Norfolk, VA, through the bay. I followed the intercoastal waterway, a channel of water that runs all the way down the east coast of the US. I was in that waterway until I got about halfway through North Carolina. That's when I headed out into the open ocean, still moving south.

The wind and the waves, the cold air and the colder nights, all of it felt like what I was looking for. Being on my own, sleeping on the boat, sailing slowly south with no real destination in mind gave me a sense of calm and freedom I had been lacking. Of course, I kept a ton of drugs and alcohol on the boat, so I was still dependent, but being alone felt really good.

I came to a large sound at one point, like a bay, and I had to cross it, which normally wouldn't have been a problem except for the soupy fog that covered the water. It started raining through the fog, and I could barely see the end of my boat. I had satellite and radio contact, but I didn't have radar, so I couldn't see where the other boats were.

This particular stretch of water is a shipping channel, and I started worrying about what I might run into. I could have easily smashed into something, anything, out there in the soup. I took me hours to make my way across the channel, and I kept following my GPS. I wasn't afraid of getting lost, but I couldn't see a thing.

After a few hours, I was through.

I headed out into the ocean again, crossed down along the Georgia coast, and when I got close to Savannah I decided to head in towards the shore for an evening. Every night on the trip I'd find an inlet and dock up. So when I found a waterway that meandered into a protected bay, I pulled into the middle of it and threw both anchors into the water. It was late at night, around 10pm.

The stars were out that night, and I spent some time laying on the boat, staring up at the stars. I thought a lot about my life on that trip. Where I had been, where I was headed. The weather was warm and a salty sea breeze came in off the ocean. I breathed in that air and it was peaceful. I went down into the small cabin of the boat and went to bed. Everything was fine. It was just another night on the water.

At some point in the middle of the night, the boat pitched and I rolled out of bed, landing on the floor with a thud. I woke up, shocked. The wind howled around the boat, and I stumbled to the door, then up onto the deck. The boat was slanted at an unnatural angle. I stared into the darkness, trying to see what was going on.

I was marooned.

A storm must have come through when I was asleep, pulling my anchors loose and pushing me up against the shoreline. Then the tide went out. There I was, the boat up against muddy land, the tide receding into the ocean. Everything leaned so far to one side that I thought the boat might roll over. I braced myself against the side and looked around the bay for someone who might be able to help, but there was nothing. No lights. No houses. I was all alone, in the middle of complete darkness.

I jumped off the boat and landed in two feet of mud. *Oh, man,* I groaned to myself. I wanted to tie the boat off to something so that it would stand up until the tide came back in, but there was nothing close enough. No trees, no structures, nothing. Just me, the boat, and a lot of mud. I knew I had to get it back into the water.

I ran further in the shore to dry land, the mud nearly yanking my shoes off. I had to take huge steps just to get through the deep mud. I found a log I could carry and waded back out to the boat. I shoved the log under the boat as best as I could and put my entire weight on it, pushing, wedging, pushing some more.

I managed to move the boat a few inches at a time.

That's what I did for the next hour, back and forth, from the front of the boat to the back of the boat. Stick the log in as deep as it would go, lean on it, push the boat a few inches into water, and then repeat at a different spot. By the time the boat was back in water that was deep enough, I was exhausted to the point of barely being able to stand up.

I somehow managed to climb back into the boat and tried to start it.

Nothing.

The boat wasn't moving. The engine wasn't

turning over.

That boat always started! I never had any trouble with it, and I knew I had plenty of battery power because I had hooked up a bunch of extra batteries before I left Maryland. So I had to go back down. I opened the compartment for the motor and looked around. I tapped the starter and, lo and behold, the boat started right up after that.

Now it was time to figure out how to clean up. I was covered in mud. The boat was covered in mud. Everything was covered in mud. I checked my GPS and saw there was a marina not too far away. It was still dark at this point, though the sun was starting to light up the eastern sky. I pulled the boat into the marina and found a water house along one of the docks.

I stripped down bare naked after making sure no one was around, and I washed myself off, and when I finished cleaning off I got dressed and went to work on the boat. I finally went to sleep around ten that morning. What a night.

A few days later, I stopped at Amelia Island just inside Florida's coastline and stayed there for a few more days. All this time, my employees were running the salvage yard on their own and doing a fine job.

That's one thing I never had to worry about. I had good people taking care of things when I was gone. Besides, a lot of the work I did could be done on the Internet, things like buying trucks for the salvage yard, or for resale. So I was still buying trucks and telling the guys where to go to pick them up. I did a lot of business while I was out on the boat.

The weather at Amelia Island was beautiful, and I went far out into the ocean, further than I'd ever gone before. Once I got out into the open, I headed south again, and I even thought about cutting over to the Bahamas. It was a 44-mile trip. I was feeling carefree and enjoying the adventure of it all. I thought I could do anything.

The problem was, I was in the Bermuda triangle, and you hear all kinds of horror stories about that place. I had studied it a lot before I left and read about it on my way down, and what happens is the water current flows north, so that's why the waters there are warm. They're coming out of the deep Caribbean. But when the wind blows to the south and meets the warm water coming north, it creates waves that are short and choppy and can be very dangerous. As long as the winds are coming out of the south, blowing north, you're okay, but otherwise it can cause some trouble, especially to a small boat like mine.

I was too scared to cross on my own, so I went south to West Palm Beach and Jupiter Beach, as far down as Fort Lauderdale. I hung out there for about a month, trying to find happiness. Trying to find a life that was different than the one I had up in PA.

But still, my life was so empty, and eventually it caught up to me. I could only run for so long. The peace and quiet I found in the sea couldn't keep my problems at bay forever. I hated myself. I hated everything. And while the trip gave me some semblance of happiness, there was still a deep unease, a deep sense that things were not as they should be.

Even though my employees did a great job, I still needed to go back from time to time. At one point while I was staying in Florida, I grabbed a rental car and drove to the airport. I turned in the rental car and headed to the security line, but when I was only six people from the front of the line, I had this strange realization.

I had my 9mm pistol in my pants. I was emptying my pockets when I realized it. What was I going to do?

I grabbed my things, stuffed them into my pockets, took my bag off the conveyor belt, and went back outside. I tried to do it all slowly – I didn't want to bring any unnecessary attention to myself. I quietly moved away from the security line. I had a few hours before my flight left, so time wasn't an issue, but where was I going to store this gun for the next few days until I returned?

I went back over to the rental car company and begged them to let me have my car back for ten minutes, the one I had just returned.

"We can't do that without renting you another car," the lady said, unsure of herself.

"I just need it for ten minutes!" I said, pointing over at the car I had parked not too long before. "Look, right there it is! I'll even leave my wallet here with you."

We went back and forth. She finally gave in.

"I am definitely not supposed to do this," she said, handing me the keys.

I had met a guy through my marijuana-supplying Jamaican friend, a guy who lived behind the airport, so I knew the area fairly well. I drove about three miles to a back road that cut into some woods. I had a bag in my backpack, so I stuck the gun in the plastic bag and buried it behind a tree I thought I'd be able to remember.

Then I returned the car and made my flight. A few days later, when I came back to Florida, I found my gun safe and sound.

After that short trip home, I returned to Florida and my boat, still looking for greener pastures, as I was always doing. But you don't find true peace that way. I didn't realize that all I was doing was running.

I had a customer in Costa Rica who bought a lot of truck parts from me. This was a legitimate business man – I'd fill entire tractor trailers with parts and sell him the whole load. He'd either drive them or ship them to Costa Rica, from one of the ports close to Philadelphia. He did this because he had a business fixing trucks and did work for people all over Central and South America.

Anyway, through the years we became good friends, and he used to beg me to come to Costa Rica to visit him. One day, when I was still in Florida on my boat trip, I thought, you know what, I'm going to go see this guy.

So, I went.

I took the next flight I could get, and as soon as I was there I loved it. The climate was warm, the people were friendly, the coffee was fresh and delicious. People who know I go to Costa Rica ask me all the time where they should go when they're there, and I always say, "I have no idea. The whole place is amazing. Just go and explore." You have the mountains and the volcanoes, the rainforests, the Pacific Ocean, and the Caribbean. You just can't go wrong. I loved it from the first time I was there. It's one of my favorite places on Earth.

I stayed for only two weeks on that first trip at a weekend getaway my friend owned. It was like a cabin, and he called it his ranch house. It was at the edge of a jungle area, and he said I could stay as long as I wanted to. I rented a car and used it as my hopping off point to other areas. He was very generous to let me stay there, and we became good friends.

While I was there, I stumbled onto a festival where the locals in a particular town get together with 700-some horses and go for an all-day ride. I got in on this; someone gave me a horse to use, and I rode along with them. We went through farmers' ranches and on back roads. Three times we crossed rivers and eventually came to a huge pasture with a fence all the way around it. That's where we tied up the horses and had a party.

It was a wonderful time, and I met so many new people. It felt like a real getaway, especially since I was so desperate for something new. I couldn't imagine feeling any further from home than I did in that field, having ridden a horse all day, celebrating life with complete strangers. And that's really all that I wanted most of the time, to get away.

One of the days I was in Costa Rica, I went to Montezuma, a hippy town on the Pacific coast at the very end of a peninsula that sticks out into the ocean. I spent three days down there, wandering the streets, meeting new people. Again, I felt like I had somehow left my troubles behind me.

But that was only wishful thinking. The reality was that no matter where I went, my old life followed me. The loneliness, the sense that something wasn't right, and the drugs. There were always drugs. That's one thing I learned in all of my travels – no matter where you are on Earth, if you want drugs bad enough, you will find them.

I walked the streets of Montezuma and there were all these little shops selling t-shirts or little knick-knacks, and I could smell the marijuana smoke floating out onto the street. Costa Rica has a lot of drugs coming out of Columbia, arriving by sea, and then making their way overland to Mexico. Because of this, the access to drugs is everywhere.

I wrote a song about my time there:

> *I sailed out of Fort Lauderdale*
> *Crossed over oceans of blue water*
> *I ended up a wreck in Costa Rica*

Where I made a hippie friend in Montezuma
He said, "Son, let me share with you a secret,
Don't waste your time like all the people
That go around dreamin' to live.
Go on and live your dream.

It didn't matter where I went during that point in my life: I would find drugs. Six months before that trip, I had been in Belize for ten days. No matter where I went, I found cocaine. It's like an international currency or something.

My Costa Rican friend down there was after me the whole time to get a business started down there. He knew the ins and outs of the trucking business, and he knew there was a lot of money to be made. I said no at first, simply because I had so many things going and didn't want to add to my responsibilities, but after a few years of him hounding me, I gave in and opened a business selling trucks and truck parts.

When I came back from that first trip to Costa Rica, I spent about a month in PA. I had left my boat in Florida, but once the weather up north warmed up, I went back down and brought the boat back to Maryland. That was a pretty quick trip. Coming home is never as romantic as heading out. I made good time. Heading north on the water reinforced the idea that there was no real escape from the life I had created. It was what it was.

A few years later, I shipped the boat to Costa Rica so I'd have something down there for my visits, and the house I stayed at was on a lake close to a volcano. When I had the boat on the lake, when I was out on the water, I could get around to the back of the volcano. I spent a lot of nights down there on the water, sleeping on the boat behind the volcano. The last time it erupted was in 1967, but whenever I went down there I could see red sparks and a glowing sky. Sometimes when I woke up in the morning, the boat would be covered in a gray ash, and every so often I heard rocks rumbling in the night. There was something amazing about that, being on a boat so close to a volcano.

That whole period of my life, that winter boat trip and the ensuing months in Costa Rica, is a time I will never forget. It was refreshing at the time, something I needed. It brought me real relief from all the angst in my life. I was under a lot of pressure in those days, with all my businesses going on and being involved in selling drugs. I had a lot of customers to keep happy, and a lot of money flowing here and there, and a lot of deadlines.

I also had a lot of personal problems – trying to

figure out what to do with my family, missing my kids, knowing that my addictions were spiraling out of control, but doing everything I could to ignore that fact. There was so much turmoil in my life during those years, and just to be alone out there on the water, floating along, the wind on the waves and the sound of the water, well, it was a peaceful place to be.

But before I knew it, everything went back to normal. Everything just went back to the same old thing. That peace I found out on the water wasn't a lasting kind of peace at all, so it wasn't the peace I was looking for.

There was real peace out there to be found. I just didn't know it at the time.

I continued dealing drugs, but on a small scale. It wasn't anything major.

But in 2008, late in the year, I bought a salvage yard up in northern PA. The owner was kind of like me, with a few illegal things going on the side. He got caught switching VIN plates on trucks. He'd take a truck that was stolen and swap out its VIN numbers and plates with a truck that had been wrecked. Then he'd sell the truck. He'd take the stickers off the wrecked truck and put them on a stolen truck. He ended up in jail and then died in prison, so I bought the salvage yard from his estate.

I had some folks up there running the place for me, employees who worked hard and I could trust. That's one thing I was good at – selecting the right people to run my businesses once I got tired of doing it myself. But my involvement in drugs, both the selling and the using, was getting deeper. I was starting to come into contact with some major players, and the stakes were getting higher.

The thing is, when you start to get involved in that dark underworld of drugs, and if you can go long enough without overdosing or ending up in prison, you start to make contacts with people who need to have things done. A friend will say, "You should talk to so-and-so," and when you do, that person will tell you, "I know someone who's looking for some help. You should talk to them." Eventually, you can end up talking to some people with connections to the very top.

I can't remember how it all came about, but I started doing some work for drug traffickers who were working in cooperation with a drug cartel in NYC. That's right, a little Mennonite boy found his way to the high stakes table. There was big money involved. The truth is, I was in so far over my head, I can barely explain it to you. But there I was.

Trucks came into town carrying tons of heroin and cocaine from Texas, the drugs hidden in the walls of the trailer and bound for New York City. We rented out entire buildings, places big enough to pull a tractor trailer inside, and then these drivers would show up in their rigs. They'd pull the tractor trailer into the building, leave it there for a few days, and then we'd go to work.

We'd take the walls out of the trailer, and in that thin space between the interior wall and the exterior shell of the trailer, there were drugs. Millions of dollars' worth of drugs. We took out the drugs and put the walls back together. We waited. Drivers would start to show up over the next few days, taking relatively small amounts of the shipment into the city. They came every few days, put more in their car, and drove east.

Each time they came back, they brought cash - stacks of cash. And we'd shrink-wrap the bills and packed them into the empty wall cavity of the trailer. When all the cash was back, we'd reinstall the walls, fill the trailer with some truck parts, and a driver would show up to drive the money back to Texas. No one ever knew the difference. No one ever had a clue about what was going on.

Before I knew it, I was caught up in it completely. A few times a month these tractor trailers would pull into town, and a few buddies and I would take out the drugs over time, replacing the drugs with the cash the drivers brought back. When all the money was back, we put the walls back in place, then stood back and watched it drive away. They paid me good money to take care of it for them. Not that I was ever entirely sure who "they" were.

I felt something then for the first time, something I hadn't felt at any other point during my descent. I felt nervous. I felt like we would get caught. It suddenly seemed like I was in way over my head, and I had this sense that the authorities were getting close, that someone was going to find out what was going on. It felt like it was time to get out.

But there was no way out.

Before, when I was dealing marijuana, that was small stuff. I could have told my Jamaican friend I was finished and he would have shrugged, found someone else, and left me alone. But the people we were dealing with now? There was no way out. There was no escape. I couldn't stop it.

And it was about to get worse.

CHAPTER SIX
TURNING BAD MONEY INTO GOOD

One day I was working around the salvage yard, just taking care of things at my desk, going over paperwork and payroll, and doing the things I didn't enjoy but had to be done. One of my employees came into the office and said someone was there to see me, so I went out into the customer area.

A man stood at the counter. His skin was very dark and his eyes were very white.

"I would like to meet with you in private," he said in a quiet voice. He had a thick African accent.

I knew something was going on. We arranged a place to meet, and in an hour I drove there. We met in Hazleton. There were two black men there when I arrived, brothers, and they had quite the story.

They said their father was involved in gold mining in an African country. He also owned oil wells there, and in the early 90s he made some deals with some people very high up in the US government. He currently had 40 million dollars in American cash, but the problem was that he had been paid with cash that was never officially in circulation, so technically it was bad money. It couldn't be used.

They showed me a few $100 bills, and I could tell it wasn't real. There was something about it. Maybe it was the paper, maybe it was the smell. I couldn't tell. I wasn't a currency expert, but I believed their story. Everything they said seemed to line up, and the obviously bad currency only led me closer to belief.

"This is the money our father has," they said.

They explained to me that there's a final process the American government does when it's printing money, and for some reason their money had never gone through that process. That's why it was still bad money. But they had figured out a way to bypass the process and make their bad money good. They just needed some help.

"You take this bad money," one of the brothers said, holding up the $100 bill, "and you spray it with a chemical. Then you take a good $100 bill, put the two together, and run an iron over them. It transfers the chemical permanently to the bad money, making it good money. You have to do it on each side, on each bill. A good $100 bill can only be used once."

I wasn't sure what to think.

"So what do you want from me?" I asked.

"We need good money so that we can make our father's bad money good. We don't have enough cash right now. If you provide good money for us to do this, you can have the good money back and we'll split whatever bad money is made good."

Later, they would also offer me a lot of money to go with them back to Africa and help them smuggle diamonds into the country. Fortunately, that never happened, though for a time I was very close to going along with it.

"If you can bring in $10,000 in cash to help us make the bad money good, we'll split it with you. You get your $10,000 back plus $5,000."

I still wasn't sure. It sounded too good to be true. Free money, basically. I knew that didn't exist.

"We'll show you."

So they took eight $100 bills of their own, the ones that were bad, and we got eight $100 bills from the bank. They sprayed on their chemical. They ironed the bills together. I took the bad money to three different banks and asked the tellers if they could confirm for me if these $100s were legitimate.

Every single bank said the same thing.

"Yes, those are good."

I was convinced. The wheels in my mind started to turn. This could be big.

There was a house I rented in a community close to my salvage yard. The community was gated, and it was called Eagle Rock. One of my employees rented it with me, and it became a place where we did our drug deals and conducted other shady activity. So we planned, along with the African brothers, to meet there on a weekend. They would bring the bad money and we'd bring the good money. We'd sit there and iron it all weekend and then we'd split the profit.

But how much money should we do?

My friend and I started talking, trying to decide how much we could pull together that weekend. We decided to do $50,000. If we brought that much, we'd make $25,000 in profit. In one weekend. We'd keep the money in the safes we had in the basement. We'd have to keep a close eye on the African brothers, but they seemed genuine, and at this point their story seemed to pan out. Whenever I doubted their story, I thought about the bank tellers who had looked over the ironed bad money and told me they were good $100 bills.

But the longer we thought about it, the greedier we got. If we're going to do $50,000, why not do $100,000? That was only 1,000, $100 bills, an amount we could easily iron in a weekend. Less than that. We could probably do that much in less than a day. It seemed like free money, and we got more and more greedy.

Then we looked at each other with wide eyes.

We remembered we had a truck sitting in the lot waiting to leave for Texas with $2.2 million in the walls. The drug cartel's cash. I could picture it sitting there, shrink-wrapped, the truck ready to go. We could use some of their money over the weekend and put it back when we were finished. No one would ever know we used it. No one would know the difference. By the time the driver came to pick up the truck early the next week, the cash would be replaced and we'd be that much richer.

We talked to the cartel's truck driver, and he went in on it with us. We'd all split the profit. We went into the truck and started taking the walls out. I was nervous. This wasn't our money, and if the cartel found out what we were doing…well, I didn't even want to think about it. Our screw guns hummed and the walls leaned out, revealing the bales of cash.

When you have large amounts of cash like that,

and it's in bags and shrink-wrapped, well, a million dollars of hundred dollar bills sits in a stack about four feet high. That's one way of estimating the amount quickly. Just a single stack.

We looked at each other. I don't even know who suggested it. At first someone said, "Maybe we should do $200,000." Why not? By the time we left the truck, we had $1 million with us. $1 million of someone else's money.

What could go wrong?

I felt the weight of the situation as I got in the car Friday night with the guy who worked with me at the salvage yard, plus the truck driver, supposed to be leaving on Monday, driving all of that cash down to Texas. There was only the three of us, plus the two African guys. The neighborhood was dark when we pulled in, and I got out of the vehicle before we got to the house. I wasn't going to show my face. I was going to wait in the woods with my gun and shoot anything that moved.

I was very worried about getting ripped off, so I figured I would wait outside and keep an eye on things. I spent my time there in the woods doing two things: making sure someone didn't show up and take our money, and thinking about everything I would be able to do with my portion.

While I was outside, my two guys were inside all night long, counting money, counting money, counting money. They spent all those hours spraying bills and ironing them. We were very organized: we kept the cartel's money that we brought in one safe, and it went straight back in there when it was used. Our half of the bad money made good went into a different safe. The Africans half went into another safe.

The hours passed quietly. I stared into the darkness. I didn't sleep for even a second.

It didn't take very long, and it was still dark by the time they ran out of the spray. My guy drove them back to their apartment in NYC so that they could get some more of the chemicals, then come back to Hazleton to finish. So they took their 500k of bad money made good out of their safe, bagged it up, and left.

I wasn't with him. The Africans got out of his car with their bag of money, and they never came back. When he came back, we convened at the house to divide the money between the three of us. I went over to the safe and opened it, the one that was supposed to have the $1 million we "borrowed" from the drug cartel.

The safe was empty.

We opened the other safe, the one with the bad money we had made good.

It fell apart in our hands. If you picked it up and rolled it into a ball, it crumbled into pieces. It was garbage.

Garbage.

Somehow, those African guys had tricked my friends, moved the good money into different spots. Somehow, they had made off with the $1 million in good money. We stared at each other. I was so angry with those African men that I wanted to kill them. Now what would we do? I was a dead man.

At first, I wanted to go to New York and hunt those guys down, but we had no idea where to find them. Surely, they wouldn't be anywhere close to where my friend had dropped them off. By now, five or six hours later, they would have vanished into the city. Or left and went somewhere different entirely. They were gone, and so was the money.

What were we going to do? The three of us sat down and talked about it. We were $1 million in the hole to a drug cartel. None of us had access to that kind of cash, not in a day. Probably not in a year. Probably never. The truck was supposed to be heading south with that money in its walls on Monday morning, and the driver was standing there, probably in a worse spot than any of us.

We decided what we would do.

First, we went back to the trailer and took out the rest of the cash: $1.2 million. We took the money out and hid it. I don't think we stopped looking over our shoulder the entire time. The truck driver especially. He was the one who was supposed to be driving south with the money.

On Monday morning, he left for Texas as he normally would have. The schedule was for him to return with the cash and pick up another load of drugs to bring north. He got out to Carlisle in central PA at a truck stop, pulled up to a fuel island, shut off his truck, locked it and went inside to get a cup of coffee.

When he came out, his truck was gone.

Of course, we were the ones who "stole" it.

The other guy working with me had gone with him and hid underneath his bunk. He had a spare key, and he took off. I was ready for him at the salvage yard in Bethel, and I had all of my guys ready and waiting. I took a crane with a huge grapple on it and a shear to cut steel, and within thirty minutes that entire truck and trailer were in pieces that we loaded into two dump trucks and shipped off to a shredder.

I called the owner of that business, in Reading,

PA.

"Listen, I've got two dump trucks coming to your place, and I want them dumped straight into the shredder. I don't want them in a pile. I don't want them sitting around. I want them dumped into the shredder, immediately."

The dump trucks got there, backed up, and dropped their cargo into the shredder. From the time the truck and trailer pulled out of the truck stop in Carlisle to the time the truck was completely shredded, basically erased from the planet, was less than two hours.

They still pinned it on us. Somehow, they knew that we had been responsible. I looked over my shoulder everywhere I went. I jumped at every shadow.

They started with the driver, taking him away and torturing him until he told them what had happened. And from him, all the blame came back on me and my friend. They came looking for me, but the thing is, they didn't have much information on me. I had never given them my real name. I had never met directly with any of them. The truck driver was the only one I ever saw.

But they knew about this other property I had, and they'd show up there from time to time, looking for me, asking my employees where I lived, where I was staying. In the middle of the night, they would break down the front door of the apartment and search the place while I slept at a motel or in one of the salvage trucks. My neighbor tried to take my picture, and I smashed the camera because I knew they had asked him to get a photo of me so that they knew exactly who they were looking for.

They didn't find me because I was hiding. I hid for a long time. I slept in broken down trucks parked in the salvage lot, back in their sleeper sections. Or I'd stay in hotels for a week or two using alias names. Or I'd leave the area for weeks at a time and my employees ran my businesses.

I was terrified.

This went on for months.

CHAPTER SEVEN
RETURNING TO CHURCH

Seeing that money gone from the safe was the worst feeling of my entire life. I thought my life was over. I don't think the bad money they brought with them ever turned to good money. I think the hundred dollar bills they gave me early on were always good hundreds, so when I went around to banks to check them out, of course they were good. We had been swindled, and we had fallen for it hook, line, and sinker.

I think if my guys in the house would have realized the African men were cheating them, if they would have tried to do something about it, I think the Africans would have shot and killed them in order to keep that million dollars. They probably would have all been dead right on the spot.

I had a lot of time to think over these things

while I was hiding, wondering if someone would find me, wondering if I would survive the week, or the weekend, or the evening. I was so alone at that point. Everyone I knew and loved from my childhood had given up on me. I had my drinking buddies, but what are they? How long do they hang around? They're with you when you're drinking, but after that most of them vanish. I was at a low point in my life, wondering if someone was going to show up and kill me, wondering what happened to all of my friends, wondering how I had gotten so low in my life, wondering why I was trapped in a cycle of alcoholism and drug abuse.

I was in the middle of the worst nightmare of my life.

Then my mother called.

I had not seen my parents for at least three years. There are a lot of reasons I didn't go by their house: I knew they didn't agree with the way I was living; I didn't like feeling guilty about the choices I was making; I knew they'd try to convince me to come back to their church; and, during that particular time of my life, I was going through something that was really tough, something I didn't want to talk to anyone about.

When my mom called, I was at one of the lowest points of my life.

Quite a few years earlier, my parents had helped

a young man get into a drug rehab program. He was about six years younger than me. He went through the program, got married, and ended up living out in Indiana close to the rehab center. He recovered from his addiction and went on to live a good life. Well, he happened to be in town and my mom thought it would be good for me to talk to him.

"Our friend is in town," she told me on the phone. "He and his wife are in the area. He's going to stop in here on Saturday night to say hello and I wish you'd come down. He'd like to meet you. It's been many years since he's seen our family."

I hadn't seen my parents in so long, and my mom really pushed me to come over. I thought this might be a good time to catch up with them, as well as see this friend of ours. On Saturday afternoon, I went down to their place and our friend was there. He and I ended up sitting under the pavilion, just the two of us, for probably two hours.

If I had ever talked to anyone who knew the situation I was in, it was him. He tried to encourage me, tried to convince me I needed to get into a program like Teen Challenge, but I didn't want that. I wasn't ready for that. I was definitely tired of my life and was ready for something different. I was ready to make some kind of a change. But I didn't want to go through something quite like that. I guess I wanted to change on my own terms, which never works, but that's where I was at.

My talk with him had a big effect on me. When I got home I decided to stay home, not leave the apartment. This was very unusual for me on a Saturday night. Usually on the weekends, I needed to be out there numbing my pain, surrounding myself with other people and noise and that kind of thing. I didn't like staying home by myself like that.

But that night, I stayed home. I drank alone, trying to float my troubles away.

At some point during this dark, lonely evening I fell asleep on the sofa. As the night went on, a storm began raging inside of me. In my sleep I felt unsettled and anxious. I was sweating, and tossing and turning. I woke up at one point so full of rage that I wanted to flip the sofa upside down and destroy the room. I was never deliberately a Satan worshiper, but I was living for Satan without knowing it. Everything I did was for myself. Every choice I made was for that moment.

But Satan knew his time with me was limited. He was trying to torment me. It was a horrible night. I felt like there were demons everywhere, all around me, inside of me. I felt like my life was imploding. But that night I sensed a fear in them; they were scared. I was scared. Something had to break. Something had to give.

That night was one of the most intense, miserable, lonely nights of my life.

I woke up the next morning in a daze from the night before. I didn't know what to think about how that night had gone, so I went and had a couple of drinks for breakfast. Then I went back to the sofa. After the night that had passed, I felt numb and disturbed.

Eventually, I peeled myself off of the sofa and went out into the morning air. I figured I'd hop on my motorcycle and go for a ride like I did almost every Sunday morning. I'd find my buddies and we'd hit the road, and then that afternoon and evening we'd end up in a bar somewhere and I could hopefully drink away my troubles again.

But as I walked outside, instead of heading towards my motorcycle, I went over and got into my car. I sat there for a moment, not really sure what was going on. I just sat there in the driver's seat, thinking about my life, thinking about everything I'd been through. I turned the key in the ignition and pulled out into the lane. The gravel driveway gave way to a long, smooth Sunday drive. I had no idea where I was going.

I drove down Schubert Road and the sun was shining through the trees. I opened my window and the air rushed through the car. Something was happening—something different.

I came to a church and something I can't explain led me to drive down the driveway. I pulled into the parking lot and parked, sitting there staring at the church. What had taken me there? Why had I gotten in my car instead of on my motorcycle?

Then something else kicked in. I turned around and left.

I drove back down the road to the Midway Diner and ate some breakfast and drank some water. The battle was still raging inside of me, though it wasn't as obvious. I didn't have the urge to turn over the furniture in the diner. But it was all in my mind. The battle was taking place. I couldn't stop thinking about that church. Somehow, I knew there was something in there for me— something crucial. So I went back.

By then a lot of cars were pulling into the parking lot. People were getting out of their vehicles and walking towards the church. It was a big, modern day Pentecostal church. It was built in 2000, only two miles from my apartment, but I never even knew it was there. I sat there for another few minutes watching all the church people head into church. I felt very much out of place. But I couldn't turn away. I got out of my car and walked inside.

I could tell some of the people were looking at me rather strangely, and I couldn't blame them for that.

I had a very rough night, was hung over and strung out, and probably didn't look that great. I felt like I was in serious need of a drink or a fix, or both. But I walked straight past everyone and went inside. I walked straight through the entrance without looking at or talking to anyone. I sat down in the back row and waited.

I kept wondering what I was doing there. I kept wondering how I had ended up in this church I had never seen before on a Sunday morning perfectly suited for riding a motorcycle. I started to think about leaving. I started gathering myself to go.

A guy came over and said hello, introduced himself. His name was Brian. He wanted me to sit up front with him.

"No," I said. "That's okay. Thanks. I'll stay here at the back."

"Come on," he said. "Join me."

"No, no," I said. "I'm okay right here."

But he just kept pressing me. He was very kind about it. Eventually I had to give in.

"I wish you would," he said. He was persistent! So I got up and walked with him all the way to the front, along the side.

It was a surreal experience. What was I doing there? How had I even arrived there? I felt like I was watching myself from the outside. I watched myself walk all the way to the front of the church with this Brian, and I sat there and waited to see what would happen next. Everything around me was calm and normal, but inside of me I felt this massive building of something, the way a tidal wave gathers in the ocean before racing towards shore.

They had a group up front that started playing music. I had never been in a church with a worship team before – all I had ever experienced was hymn singing. The band started playing and I wondered if they were having a concert that morning. I had never heard anything like it before. But there was something very cool there, something genuine. People seemed to be happy showing up as they were. It's hard to explain. I relaxed a little bit. I felt my shoulders loosen up. Maybe I would be okay.

But my head was still pounding through my hangover. I kept thinking back through the previous night, the battle that had raged inside of me, the sense that I might explode if things didn't change. Then something started to happen. I know now it was the Spirit of God surrounding me, but at the time I didn't know what was going on.

All I knew was that I suddenly started weeping, and I couldn't stop. I sat there and I cried and I cried. I was bawling. Sweat poured out of me, as if my body was doing everything it could to get rid of the poison, get rid of the dirt, and get rid of my past. I think the carpet was wet underneath me. My hair dripped with sweat. And I kept crying. I couldn't stop.

At some point the pastor came over to where I sat and started talking to me, praying with me. Then other men came around and prayed with me. I was a wreck. I was an absolute wreck. I can't remember anymore what anyone said to me that morning or what they prayed over me; I just remember crying my eyes out.

Words started pouring out of my mouth, ideas that had begun to form in the deepest parts of my soul but that I had not yet spoken. A deep desire for change welled to the surface.

"I'm done," I whispered to God. "I'm finished. I don't want to live like this anymore."

The service came and went. The people in the church left, went home. And still I sat there. I didn't know what else to do. I felt like I was ready to make a new beginning, but how would I do that? Where would I go live? What kind of a life was I looking for? I had too many questions and very few answers. It was all very overwhelming.

Below everything was the question, "Does God really love me?" But as I sat there in the church, I remembered a Bible verse from my childhood.

"For God so loved the world that he gave his only begotten Son, that whosoever believes in him will not perish but have eternal life…"

John 3:16. I remembered it, after all those years.

Ted Williams, the pastor, came back over to me. The church was nearly empty.

"Will you come to my house for lunch?" he asked, and I agreed. I went with him to his house and I spent all day there. A few other people joined us, folks from the church who understood what I was going through, people who could speak good things into my life. I think it was well after 10pm before someone brought me back to the church for my car.

That Sunday changed my life forever. This is the thing, and it's hard to believe, but it's true: I never touched a drug after that Sunday morning. My desire to do drugs, my body's dependency on them to function, it was all gone. *Immediately*. I can't even explain it.

That was the summer of 2010. Everything changed after. Everything I had ever done wrong started catching up to me. It was time to reckon with the life I had created.

Within a few months of my transformation, the cartel finally caught up with my friend at the salvage yard up state, the guy I worked with, the guy who had tried to help me work the African deal. He and his wife were in the office doing some paperwork, and all of a sudden there were guys all around them with guns pointed. The men grabbed him, shoved him into a car, and took off. His wife called me and told me what had happened. She was hysterical.

"What are we going to do?" she asked. "We have to do something!"

She only knew a small part of what we were involved in. She never knew the extent of it, at least not that I was aware of.

"I don't know," I said, sitting down, worried sick. "What can we do?"

They returned him, but not without conditions.

The group of men with guns had taken him to New York, where they vanished into dark streets and alleyways. Eventually they took him down into an underground room, chained him to a post, and put a gun to his neck.

"Tell us where the money's at," the leader said to him.

Well, we had hidden the money, buried it, and we didn't know what else to do with it. We kept it in hiding for a time, but later we tried to appease them by returning it.

He shook his head.

"I don't have it."

"Either you tell us where it's at, or we're going to kill you," the man said in a quiet voice.

"I don't have it. I don't know where it is. Just get it over with. Just kill me," he said.

"Where's the guy you're working with?"

"Just kill me!" he begged.

This went on for quite some time, with them holding a gun to his head and him begging them to do it, to get it over with.

One of the men left and came back in. He had photographs, and he held them up one at a time in front of the man. They were photos of his five children. Then they showed him photos of his mom and dad.

"You have two weeks to bring in your buddy, as well as the money we're missing. If you don't, we'll start killing your children, one at a time, until they're all dead. Then we'll kill your parents. Then, when everyone you love is dead, we'll kill you."

So it all came back on me.

What would you do?

I went in to talk to my pastor, Ted Williams. I

went in and spilled the whole thing to him, the drugs I had been selling, the cash we had been smuggling, and the cartel I was involved with. When I finished telling him the story he sat there for a moment. It was very quiet. Finally, he spoke.

"You have to call the FBI," he said. "You don't have any options."

I shook my head.

"I can't call them!" I exclaimed. "They have moles all over the place. Half of them are paid off by the cartels. I can't. If I do, I'm as good as dead."

"You have to," he said. "You don't have any other options."

"I make one call to them and the cartel will know exactly who and where I am. The FBI is paid off. The NYPD is paid off. Everyone is. I can't go to them."

"We're calling the FBI," he insisted. "You don't have any other way forward."

He called them for me, sitting there in his office. He called the Harrisburg office and they transferred him to Scranton.

"I'd like to ask you a few questions," he said, as I sat across the desk from him, shaking my head, still not sure that this was the right thing to do.

He went on to tell a little bit of my story, not giving my name. Very little information. He may have mentioned the location of my salvage yards.

"I just want to know what you can do for him," my pastor said.

But they already knew about me.

"You must have Stanley Nolt sitting in front of you," the agent said. They knew right away who he was talking about simply because of the story he told them.

The FBI begged me to come into the office.

"We won't charge you," the agent said. "Nothing like that. Just come in and talk to us."

So I went in.

CHAPTER EIGHT
LIFE AFTER ADDICTION

I was in my pastor's office on a Friday. My friend was back, and I convinced him to come with me. So first thing Monday morning, the two of us were walking up to the FBI building in Scranton.

We went in the front door and, through a little phone in the wall, we told them who we were. Several agents came to the door, immediately split the two of us up, and took us into separate rooms for questioning.

That process seemed to take forever. They asked me everything about the previous few years, and they asked me the same questions over and over again, sometimes in different wording, sometimes simply the same question. The questions came fast and furious, and I could tell they were skeptical about my answers.

"Listen, these things you're talking about, they

only happen in movies. Not real life. Do you realize how many times we have people coming in here, telling us stories like this, people who only want to make a name for themselves? These things don't actually happen."

I waited until they stopped talking.

"This is really happening," I said.

They kept us separated all day, making sure our stories lined up. My friend told them about being taken into an underground room. They made him take a lie detector test three different times that afternoon, and he passed each one. They were blown away.

They questioned us through most of the day, and when we finished they asked if we would come back in the following day.

We went back the next morning and the tone was different. I didn't feel like I was being interrogated. They were more open with us.

The agent we met with said that they had 230 FBI agents on the case related to the cartel we had gotten involved with. They had it narrowed down, and they thought they knew who the guys were who took my friend to New York.

"This is the largest Spanish cartel that's ever operated in the US," he told us.

He went on to offer us witness protection in exchange for our testimony. They wanted to meet with us for a few more days, have us tell them everything (again), and then testify in court. In exchange, they would protect us. They wanted to move us to another part of the country, maybe even another part of the world.

Would we do it?

"No way," I said. My friend said the same thing.

I had changed my life. At that point, I just wanted to get out of the whole situation. I was finished with drugs, finished with everything. I felt like testifying would thrust me right back into a world I was trying so hard to get out of.

"If I testify," I said, "it doesn't matter where you hide us. These guys are too smart. They're everywhere. They'll find us anyway. I don't want to have any part in it."

After they realized they couldn't convince me to testify or cooperate with them, the agent brought out a huge manila folder and put it in front of me. He began pulling out photographs of me, my salvage yard, all kinds of stuff. They had a ton of information on me.

"We have a lot on you," he said. "There were many times we were getting ready to move in but something would always change."

He paused, and we stared at each other.

"We're still going to get you. It's just a matter of time."

"How's that?" I asked. "You just said you don't have anything to pin on me."

"Not yet," he said. "You'll do something else. No one walks away from this for good. You'll go back to your old tricks soon enough, and when you do, we'll be waiting for you."

"Well, that's not true," I said. "My life has changed. I'm a different man."

"We'll see," he said.

This all happened in late 2010.

That's when I hid. I was terrified that these guys were going to find me. They had already found my friend, given us two weeks to give them the money. The FBI wouldn't help us unless we promised to testify, which I felt was a death sentence anyway. So I went into hiding on my own.

For three months, I never slept in the same place. I moved around. I kept to the edges of society. I was worried. I went to Florida for a week, stayed in different motels.

Then, one morning, I walked out of a motel and realized something: I was sick and tired of hiding. I didn't want to do it anymore. I walked outside. It was a beautiful day, the sun shining, the birds singing. I looked up into the blue sky.

"You know what, God?" I said in a kind of prayer. "I'm not going to hide anymore. If these guys are going to kill me, so be it. I have made things right with you, and if they kill me then I'm coming home to be with you. If you have a plan for me being in this world, then you'll have to protect me because I'm not hiding anymore. I'm not living like this anymore."

So I didn't. I stopped hiding. For a long time after that, I lived in a garage up in Bethel. I had a little garage there on my salvage yard property. That's not to say I wasn't scared anymore. Whenever I got home after dark, I'd drive around and shine my headlights in all the dark places. I'd look around for strange cars, and when I got out of my car to walk into the shop, I was a nervous wreck because I was just waiting to hear the sound of a gun going off, to feel a bullet tear through me.

I still wonder if these things will catch up with me some day.

Less than a year later, there was a huge sting and many of the men involved in that cartel were caught and locked up. That's the only explanation I have for how my friend and I fell off their radar. I don't think they got all of them, but after that they were reeling, and I was the least of their concerns.

There's a story that happened before I cleaned up my life that's important to tell. It took place in the year or so leading up to my experience at church.

One night I was hanging out in Lebanon with a bunch of friends at the Silver Dollar Saloon on 10th Street. We were over there having a pretty normal Saturday night when someone called. They said a girl we knew was getting beat up by her boyfriend. Well, I guess a couple of the guys I was with wanted to do something about so I said I'd drive them there, but that was it. I wasn't getting involved.

We drove quietly through the neighborhood on the south side of Lebanon and came up to this guy's house. His daughter was with me, and as soon as the car came to a stop she jumped out and raced inside to see what was going on.

I stayed in my pickup, parked on the street. To be honest, I could hear them shouting at each other from where I sat, and I was not going to get involved. It sounded like a war zone, and I didn't want to get mixed up in someone else's business. But for some reason I stayed there. I didn't drive off.

The fighting couple came bursting through the doors of the house and the guy was shouting like a lunatic. Then everything got crazy. Before I knew it, he was standing beside my car, sticking his face in my window, shouting at me! Well, I hadn't done anything, and I certainly wasn't going to put up with some drunk, girlfriend beater shouting in my face.

At first I didn't respond, but then he started pounding the side of my head. I'd had enough.

I reached down beside my seat and pulled out a handgun. When he saw it, he froze in place. He backed up. But I'd had enough. I was finished with this guy. I got out of my car and pushed him to the sidewalk. He was scared. I could see it in his eyes.

I took the gun and stuck the barrel up against his head, and we were frozen there in time. My finger was on the trigger. A rage flooded through me. I wanted to shoot him. To this day, I don't know why I didn't.

The police showed up.

They talked to everyone on the scene and eventually told me that what I did was okay. He had attacked me and I had a right to pull a gun to protect myself. But my gun permit was expired. Typical. I have always been terrible with paperwork.

I got charged with an expired gun permit and they took my gun. They also searched my pick-up, and that's what scared me the most because underneath my console I had stashed enough cocaine to get half of the city of Lebanon high as a kite. I sat in the patrol car in handcuffs and started to think, this is it. This is when my life finally goes south.

But all they found was a bowl used to smoke crack, so I was also charged with possession of drug paraphernalia.

What a night.

My lawyer kept buying me time, pushing things off into the future. There were appeals and motions and all manner of other things I didn't completely understand.

Then came God, sweeping into my life. I wanted to get all of this stuff behind me. I asked my lawyer if we could just wrap it up and I would do whatever I had to do, even if that meant spending time behind bars.

We went to court, finally, and my lawyer had agreed to a plea deal with the district attorney that involved me doing some jail time. God was with me, and I was okay with that outcome.

But when we went into court for sentencing, the judge had other things in mind. He commented on the amount of time that had passed since the incident, and that I hadn't been in any trouble since then. He talked about my business and the employees I hired, the people who were working because of my business. At the end of a long talk, he said one sentence.

"Stanley Nolt doesn't belong in jail."

That was that. I got 18 months' probation and had to do 90 days house arrest.

That was a long 90 days. But something happened just after that time, and I began to see how God was using every part of my story to point people to Him.

I had a friend who was with me through the toughest years. His name was Phil. But he changed his life about nine years before I did, and he'd call me every few weeks to talk to me and encourage me. He went to a little Brethren church, and at some point got to know my oldest son who told Phil he should stay in touch with me.

He never put pressure on me. He never made me feel like a bad guy. He was just there as a friend.

After God changed my life, Phil continued to support me, but he also started challenging me.

"You should come with me some Sunday night," he said. "We go into prisons and share the Good News, the Gospel of Jesus Christ."

Twice a month he did a prison chapel service at the Lebanon County jail.

"There's no way," I said. At that point, I was not comfortable talking in front of crowds of people. I couldn't even talk in front of three or four people, much less a couple hundred. That just wasn't me. Thinking about it filled me with anxiety.

Besides that, there was no way I was stepping foot in jail voluntarily. Are you kidding me? I had tried to avoid that place my entire life. Why would I walk in behind bars if I didn't have to?

But Phil wouldn't give up, and I guess he saw how I had cabin fever after serving that 90 days of house arrest.

"Why don't you come along to the prison chapel meetings we're doing?" he asked me one day not giving up.

I finally agreed.

"Okay," I said. "Fine. I'll come along and sit in the chapel, but I'm not talking in front of the group. No way!"

"No problem," he said.

We walked into the prison and I was feeling pretty nervous about the whole thing. I had spent the last few decades of my life dreading that place, feeling like I might end up there at some point. It was hard for me to relax, at least at first. But once we got inside and started hanging out with the other guys, something clicked.

I even saw a guy that I knew, someone I used to hang out with on the streets. We started talking about life and what I was up to and what he was up to and before I knew it, Phil tapped me on the shoulder.

"The hour is up," he said. "We have to go."

"What do you mean, the hour is up?" I asked him. "Didn't we just get here?"

I couldn't wait to go back again.

By the second or third time I went, I worked up the nerve to talk in front of the whole group. I was nervous, but I also felt an unexpected kind of courage. I shared my story, about that first sip of beer and where it all took me, the trouble I'd been in and how God had brought me out of it. It felt good to share the wonderful ways God had changed me. It felt very freeing.

After I spoke, a guy came up to me and introduced himself.

"Do you remember me?"

I stared at his face and tried to place him, but I couldn't.

"Can't say that I do," I said.

He laughed.

"C'mon, man," he said. "You don't remember me?"

I tried to search my memory for something but

it wasn't there. I shook my head.

"Sorry, man."

"I was the bartender at Bainey House," he said. "You know, in Myerstown?"

Then I kind of recognized him. But he didn't look anything like he used to. When he was the bartender, he had really long hair, but the guy in front of me had shaved his head.

"My goodness," I said. "What are you doing in here?"

He told me what he had done and how long he had been behind bars. We chatted for a while about people that we both knew.

"You are the Stan who had the salvage yard, right?" he asked, as if our conversation had suddenly left him in doubt as to exactly who I was."

"Yeah," I said. "That's me."

He shook his head.

"Are you for real?" he asked.

I didn't know what he meant at first.

"Did you really change your life?" he asked.

I paused. He had a hungry look on his face, as if he couldn't believe it was me, but he really wanted to believe it.

"Yeah," I said. "My life is different now."

And just like that, he started crying. Big old

tears streamed down his cheeks. He wiped them away and then gave me a huge hug. When he took a step back, he said something I'll never forget.

"If there's hope for you," he said, "then there's hope for me."

That's what he said.

Wow.

"The first two nights you came in here," he told me, "I was in the chapel every night. We guys would all go back to the cell block and, to be honest, we were all laughing about it. We were sure it was all a show, that you were faking it because you were smuggling drugs in here for someone."

"No, no, no," I protested, and we both laughed.

"You really did change your life?" he asked, his voice quiet.

"Yeah," I said. "My life is changed."

After that, going into the prisons really moved me. I saw the opportunity I had to influence those guys for good. I saw how encouraged they were to see someone who God had changed, completely.

But going into the prisons wasn't easy. Not in the least.

I walked into a prison service we were doing at the Lancaster County jail when I saw someone I recognized. It took me a minute to place him, but when I did, it all came back.

There was this guy from Myerstown who was a small drug dealer, and his day job was washing dishes at the main motel there in town, the Lantern Lodge. Anyway, he had sold marijuana for me when I was buying from the Jamaican guy at my salvage yard. Through him I got into contact with a 15-year-old kid who started selling and running marijuana for me.

This is the person I recognized in the prison. The kid I had introduced to the drug world. Except he wasn't a kid anymore – he was probably 18 or 19 years old, and he hadn't been selling for me when he got caught, but I was the one who got him started in it.

That was a hard pill to swallow, especially after I talked to him and found out what he was in prison for. It really affected me. I felt responsible for him. For one of the first times, I saw how the poor choices I had made had influenced others. The thing is, though, when you're in the middle of it, you don't really care about people enough to change the way you're living. You do what you have to do to get the next fix, the next high, or make the next sale. You'll neglect people you really love. You'll pull in folks without caring about what happens to them in the end.

Addiction is a terrible thing.

For months after God changed my life, I still kept drinking. The desire for drugs was gone, and I wasn't partying anymore. I wasn't getting drunk. But I always *had* to have a drink. I kept a six-pack in the fridge and had a beer with dinner. If I was going out on a job, maybe picking up a wrecked truck, I'd always stop on my way home and have a drink. Every day. I just had to.

In those days I was heading down to Costa Rica every so often for business with my salvage yard there. Anyway, I had a good time down there, took care of what I needed to take care of, and then came home. Once I got back, I went over to my pastor Ted's house. We became very close after God changed my life. I spent a lot of time at his house, and he was an incredible mentor for me. Still is.

Ted is probably in his 60s, born in Mexico. He's been saved for 40 years, went to seminary, and his first job out of seminary was with Teen Challenge, a Christian drug and alcohol rehabilitation program. He became a pastor there and eventually the church he pastored on Teen Challenge property became a community church.

Ted always knew how to handle me. He was always asking me, "Why did God take you to my church that morning? It was not a coincidence." He asked me that question to remind me all that God had done for me. And I was always brutally honest with Ted. I thought he deserved that from me.

Well, I came back from Costa Rica that trip on a Tuesday, and Ted and I went for a walk out Airport Road.

"I had a couple of drinks down there in Costa Rica," I confessed. We stopped in the middle of the road and he put his finger right in my face. Ted was the kind of guy who didn't beat around the bush. If he had something to tell you, he'd tell you.

"I want to tell you," he said, "that you have to quit completely. I know your kind. I worked with your kind for many years. If you don't quit completely, soon, you'll become an alcoholic again and it will retake your life. You'll lose it all again. And then what?"

"I know," I said desperately. "I want to quit. I don't want to do this anymore."

For the next few weeks, I became very serious with God when it came to my drinking. I cried out to Him.

"You took the desire for drugs away," I said. "Why can't the desire for alcohol just leave me the same way?"

I was at a point in my life where I would do

anything to stop drinking.

"God," I said, "if you take the desire for alcohol away, I will never put beer to my lips again. Never."

I don't know if that is the right thing to do or not. I don't know if making those kinds of promises, those kinds of deals are good. But I know this. Soon after that I realized it had been about three weeks since I had a drink. I kept thinking back over my days, over my nights. Surely I had had something to drink at some point? But, no, it was true.

I was clean.

I didn't go back after that. Not that there haven't been temptations.

I met up with an old friend of mine. I went by his house and the two of us sat down. Actually, he went to the refrigerator first and pulled out two Rolling Rocks —that was always his beer. He sat them down on the table in between us, the glass green and glistening. Sweat beads forming on the label. A nice cold beer.

"C'mon," he said. "Just for old times' sake. We gotta have a drink together."

You know, I could have had that beer and no one would have known except my friend and God. I never would have had to tell anyone. But God would have known, and I'd made a promise. I couldn't do it.

"No," I said. "Thanks, but I won't."

And to be honest, I didn't have a desire to. It was easy for me to say no.

There came a time when I finally knew I was finished drinking, when I knew the hold it had had on me for so many years was dead and gone. If I had any doubts, this was when I knew beyond a doubt that I was finally free.

I was involved in racing for a little while when I had my salvage yard. I was friends with the Nascar driver Jimmy Spencer, and I'd go to different races when I could. His family owns a salvage yard up in Berwick, PA, and his dad, Ed Sr. drove race cars back in the day. I did a lot of business with them, and they sort of dragged me into the racing scene. The racing world. But once I was in it, I loved every minute of it. I even ran a late model car in a couple of races.

I could see myself getting even deeper into it, and I sponsored a few cars. One of the guys I got to know during this time was named Earl. He drove the car I sponsored, and he was a good driver. We became friends.

Earl was getting married and invited me to the wedding. This was after I had experienced freedom from my drug and alcohol addictions. At first, I wasn't going to go, but it came down to the last Saturday before the wedding and I changed my mind. I thought it would be nice to see some of these old friends, guys I hadn't seen for a long time, almost a year. So I went.

I got there late, just as the service was ending. There was a race car parked outside.

"Stan's here!" my friends shouted. "Stan's here! How are you, buddy?"

Immediately, they all wanted to get me a drink. They were used to me being the drunk at the party.

"No, thanks," I said smiling. "That's okay."

Everyone was standing there outside, and there was an open bar. I stood there catching up with a couple of guys, and I glanced around. Everyone had a drink in their hand. Everyone was asking me if I wanted a drink. There was an open bar – everything was free. It was all there. All my old favorites.

There, in the midst of all of that alcohol, I finally knew I was free, because the only thing I thought was, "Even if I go over to that bar, I don't know what I'd order." Nothing sounded good to me. Nothing tempted me. It was in that moment right there, standing beside an open bar at the wedding of a friend that I knew I was delivered from beer and alcohol. Six months had passed since my covenant with God, and there I was.

I went home that night and I looked in the mirror. I stared at that face in the glass, that person who had been at a wedding and not had a single drink. I wondered if that person was really me. I could barely comprehend how far I had come.

I remembered the first beer I had when I was a kid and when that guy I was working with in the field handed me a cold beer, and then another. And then another. It felt like such a long time ago. I thought of all I had been through, all the places I'd been. I thought of my boat trip down the coast, the warm nights in Costa Rica, the fear I had felt when I was on the run. I thought about how I had tried to quit drinking, off and on, for 26 years. I stared at myself in the mirror, and it was the most incredible feeling. I was full of thanks to God. I knew, then, that it was over.

CHAPTER NINE
GOING BACK TO THE BARS AND PRISONS

One Christmas soon after that, I went around with some friends from church to the bars I used to frequent. We started taking Christmas cookies with us and give them out to people there. Ted came along, and five or six others from church. I sat down with the guys in the bar, some of them my old friends, and just talked to them. Sometimes I saw a lot of people I knew.

I sat down with an older fellow named Charlie. I knew him from my drinking days. I sat beside him and we started talking. A few of the girls at the bar turned to one of the guys who had come in with me from church.

"We don't remember the name of the guy you

came in with," one of the girls told my friend. "But he used to get drunk all the time!"

"That's true," my friend said, smiling. "You're right."

Charlie had come with me to church about four months before that night, and we had a good time catching up.

"Yeah," he said. "You know, I prayed to God. I know Him. I feel like I have a relationship with Him. But this?" And he gestured around to the bar. "This? It's all I've ever known. My whole life. I just can't fit in at church."

I tried to talk him into coming back sometime, if only to see me and say hello. We talked for about 20 minutes, and I prayed with him. As we prayed together, I saw a few tears run down his cheek.

Six weeks later I got a phone call from someone who knew Charlie. He had died. Someone found him in an old house in the mountain. Some hunters thought something didn't look right about the porch, and they found him slumped over the railing. He had always smoked pretty hard, and they figured he walked out to have a smoke when he died. I went to his funeral, and I cried for Charlie. Little did I know that when I saw him in that bar handing out Christmas cookies that I'd never see him again on this Earth.

I still remember his words to me in the bar during our final talk. I'll never forget the pain in his eyes.

"I just can't fit in at church," he said, and there was a tear rolling down his cheek.

That doesn't seem right to me.

Going into the bars like that was really hard. It wasn't that I was embarrassed to go in and witness. I'm never ashamed to tell people about everything that Jesus did for me. My life is completely different than it was, and it's all because of God. I will talk about that anytime.

The hard part about going into these bars is that it seemed like I could feel the presence of those demons, the addiction and the sadness, the despair. The drugs. It was an environment I used to practically live in, so it's hard to go back in there because it forces me to remember how low I had been. But it gets easier as time passes

One of the bars we went to in particular was a hard, old place. It just felt dark when I walked in. There was something very evil about it, and it had been one of those places I spent a lot of time in.

One Christmas we walked up to the door and I could hear a band playing inside. It brought back a flood of memories and emotions from earlier in my life. It was like someone had picked me up and set me down ten years earlier. I turned to the rest of the folks from church who were with me.

"Are you sure you want to tag along?" I asked them. I felt a lot of resistance. I wasn't even sure if I wanted to go in. If I could go in. The memories were hard to think about. The sound of people talking loudly, music playing, glasses clinking together – it all took me back.

But it's also important to realize the difference you can make in a place like that. Just going inside. I thought about my friend Charlie, and I wondered if maybe talking to him in those last weeks of his life somehow made a difference. I don't know. I guess you never know.

That's why we keep going. You never know.

So we went in and the band we had heard playing was just doing a sound check. The church folks and I mingled around for a bit. The band came up to the bar where we were hanging out, and a few of us started chatting with them. I went over to the guy who ran the sound equipment.

"Hey," I said to him. "Merry Christmas! Do you think before the band gets up to play, we could sing a few Christmas carols in here?"

"Absolutely," he said with a big smile on his

face. "Get your guys up front and take the mics."

"Oh, we don't have to have mics," I said, laughing. "We'll just stand over here beside the bar and sing loud."

"No, no, no," he insisted. "Go up to the mics." He seemed really happy about singing Christmas carols, so we took him up on his offer. A friend of mine was along who plays the guitar, so he borrowed one of the band members guitars and played. When we started singing, I wasn't sure what to expect. Would people enjoy it? Would they like singing these old carols? Or would they start booing and kick us out of the bar?

Well, it turns out everyone likes Christmas carols. Or almost everyone. Probably 3/4ths of that bar started singing with us, everyone's voices ringing out.

> *Joy to the World*
> *The Lord is Come*
> *Let Earth Receive Her King!*
> *Let Every Heart Prepare Him Room*
> *And Heaven and Nature Sing*
> *And Heaven and Nature Sing*
> *And Heaven, and Heaven and Nature Sing*

A few people even got out on the dance floor and danced around a little bit. One of the band members came up and shared the microphone with me, singing just as loud as I was. They loved it.

That night, we had church right there in the bar.

The church I went to took a team of twelve people to the Dominican Republic on a mission trip. It's a beautiful place, but that particular visit was no vacation. The entire time, we were on the streets and in the villages witnessing and helping with church services. Not to mention the long hours we did of service to the community.

I returned from that first trip, but I couldn't shake the heartache I felt for the people there who lived in such awful poverty. I had gotten out into the villages and made some new friends. They were, every single one of them, thankful for what they had. Yet I had so much more than them, at least materially speaking. I loved their hearts and wanted to keep serving them.

I started going back on my own for the next year and a half, went back seven or eight times to the same areas and helped with various things. People from there started emailing me, wondering when I was coming back.

One time while I was down there, a pastor I knew brought up the fact that there was such a huge need in the prisons. I told him I'd love to help serve the men in the prisons, that it was what I did back in the States, so he started to ask around to see if he could get me into one of the major prisons in San Juan.

The inmates in those prisons receive very little of anything. They are fed, but that's it – no hygiene stuff is given to them whatsoever. So I gathered a bunch of hygiene kits and sent them down. They included things like toothpaste and toothbrush, washcloths, that kind of stuff. I sent them down ahead of time and planned on going into the prisons and handing them out.

Well, I got down there and had all of these packages ready when the warden stepped in and stopped us.

"No way," he said. "There are no Christian services allowed in my prison of any kind."

The next day I met a doctor, and she came to the mission house and helped in giving medical services to the poor. She took care of the sick there. Well, she overheard us talking and said she happened to have an office in that very prison and went there twice a week to take care of the inmates.

"I know the warden very well," she told me. "Let me talk to him."

So she came back the next day to the mission house and said she had spoken with the warden. He gave in and said that I could go into her office in the prison, and her office only. He'd allow one inmate at a time to come in and meet with me to receive their hygiene items. That was it. No religious services.

"Okay," I said. "That's fine. At least it's something."

The three of us – it was the pastor, the doctor, and I – headed into the prison the next day along with an interpreter. We went inside and met the warden, and he had decided overnight that he would let ten inmates come into the office with me instead of just the one. I was glad to hear that. It seemed like he was softening up a little bit, thanks to my friend the doctor.

Anyway, by the time it came for me to hand out the kits and say a little bit, there were twelve inmates in the office, and the warden joined us as well. I was a little nervous at first about what he might say or do. I didn't want to get kicked out before giving out the hygiene kits, but I felt like it was time for me to tell my story. So I did.

I told them about what I had been involved in, the trouble I found, and how God changed my life. I tried to be very encouraging. I told them there was still a lot of good they could do, even while they were in prison, and how important it was to make good choices when they got back out into society so that they didn't end up back in here again. I told them they needed to cut off the ties they had with their trouble-making friends and get involved in new circles of people.

"You have to seek God in your life," I said.

Suddenly the warden stood up.

"Whoa, whoa," he said. "Stop."

And I thought he was going to kick me right out of there. I thought it might be the shortest prison ministry ever.

He came over to me, and there was a smile on his face.

"I want every person in my prison to hear what you have to say," he said. He motioned for me to follow him out of the office.

That particular prison is like a compound with a courtyard in the middle. There was one room off to the side that opened out into the courtyard. He brought out the entire prison into the courtyard, all 700 inmates. They stood in the courtyard, and some stood in the room with me. Everyone could hear me.

I gave the entire prison my testimony. Everyone listened, and the whole place was very quiet. After I finished, the warden came up to me.

"Please come back," he begged me. "You are welcome in my prison any time."

So I've been back there twice, meeting with the men and sharing my story, my perspective. That warden was friends with the warden in the Azua prison, so I got into there twice as well. That particular prison is designed for 100 inmates, but it currently houses 600. They let me visit some of the rooms while I was there, and in some cases 15 men shared a room meant for only a few. They'd all lay on the floor to sleep – no beds. In the corner of the room there was a hole with a ball sitting on top of it. That's where they go to the bathroom, in that hole, and the smell coming up is so strong that they keep a ball over the hole to plug it.

Those trips into the prisons have become very important to me. I know there are a lot of people out there doing prison ministry, but I feel a connection with those men in a way I rarely connect with anyone else.

During one of my later trips to Costa Rica, I had a friend who bought trucking parts from me and shipped it around South America. This friend lived in Nicaragua, so while I was down there I decided to try to go and see him. A friend of mine from Costa Rica went along. Turns out, getting across the border from Costa Rica into Nicaragua, at least as an American, isn't the easiest thing in the world. It took me over half a day, and it was this convoluted process where you have to hire a "customers' broker" to take your passport and get it approved. It's difficult, and time consuming.

Once we were through, we headed up to visit this guy in Grenada. It was such a beautiful town, very historic, and it sits on the edge of a lake. We got a hotel there that night in the downtown district and then went out for a walk. We got back to the room around 8pm, but by 9pm I was already feeling restless. I wasn't one bit tired. I got up and got dressed.

"Where are you going?" my friend asked me.

"I have to get out," I said. "I've got to go for a walk, or something."

"No way," he said. "It's not safe out there. You can't go out. You don't understand. This is a violent city."

This hotel we were staying in had a courtyard in the middle, so I thought I'd just go out there and walk around in circles for a little bit.

"Okay," he said, "But don't go outside. It's not safe here."

I wandered around the courtyard for a bit. It was a warm night, and dark. I stared at the front door. I walked through it, stood on the front porch. There was an armed guard there with a machine gun. He nodded at me. I nodded back. I looked down the long street and there were only one or two dim street lights – besides that, everything was dark. I walked out into the middle of the street and started walking.

Across the street from the hotel was a large park. We had strolled through that park earlier, during the day, and it was one of those parks where guys had tables set up and were selling handmade jewelry and other trinkets. During the day it had seemed lively and fun. But at night, the park was anything but that. It was dark and gave me a strange feeling. The shadows were thick.

I got about a block away from the hotel, just walking down the middle of the street, and on the left-hand side I saw a gang of guys standing on the sidewalk underneath a dim, flickering streetlight. Other than that one single light, the city was dark.

I guess they could tell I wasn't from there, and as I got closer they all started shouting for my attention.

"Yo! Yo! Where you going?" they shouted at me. They were playful at first, just giving me a hard time.

"I'm just going for a walk," I said, slowing down but not stopping. I wasn't sure if it would be a good idea to engage them directly. There were quite a few of them, and I knew they were up to no good.

"What are you looking for?" they asked, slowly moving towards me, eyeing me up.

"I'm not looking for anything," I said, smiling because I knew what they were trying to give me. "I'm just going for a walk."

"No, no, c'mon, man. What do you need? Whatever you need, we can sell it to you." A few more of them stood up from where they leaned against the building. I could tell that things were escalating.

"I'm not looking for anything," I insisted. "I'm just taking a walk."

They weren't convinced. I tried to keep walking, but before I knew what had happened, the entire group came out into the street and surrounded me. Only two of them could speak English. I stopped.

"Listen, guys," I said. "I'm not looking to buy anything."

"Aw, man, c'mon. We'll sell you something. Anything you need."

"I want to tell you something," I said. "I know what you guys are all about. I know this business. Whatever you think you're selling, I have something that's a whole lot better than what you have."

Their eyes lit up. I had their attention. At first they thought I was an American they could take advantage of – now they thought I was an American peddling better stuff than they had.

"What do you have?" they asked.

"I have Jesus Christ right here with me, and the Holy Spirit is right here with us, too."

They melted. The whole situation lost its edge.

"I used to be in this life you guys are living," I said quietly. "I understand what you're going through. But God changed my life. He protects me. He is always with me."

A few of them turned and walked away, waving their hands at me. I few stayed where they were. But I walked over to the side of the street with a couple of them and sat on the front steps of an old, vacant building. We sat there for over two hours, and different guys came and went from the park. But the main two stayed there the entire time, listening to what I had to say. They asked a lot of questions. Drug deals were going on all around us the entire time, but I ignored that and stayed focused on telling them my story, how God had changed me.

They really couldn't get enough. They wanted to hear everything. And when I talked about God, they had a look on their face, a look that said, "I hope that's not too good to be true."

Around midnight I stood up.

"I need to go back to my motel room," I said.

The two guys I had been talking with the entire night stood up with me.

"We'll walk you back to your motel."

"You don't have to do that," I said. "I'll be

fine."

"No, you're not fine," they said. "It's not safe for you to be out here. You should never have come here at night."

So they walked me back to the hotel, one on either side, like guardian angels. We chatted the entire way, like old friends. The guard was still standing there on the front steps.

Nicaragua. One of the poorest countries in Central America. They need to hear the Good News.

CHAPTER TEN
A HOME FOR THE BROKEN

After I changed my life and started seeking God, my old drinking buddies kind of vanished. I didn't go back to partying anymore, and I wasn't doing drugs, so most of my old friends weren't interested in hanging out. I spent more and more time at church. I had a lot of heart-to-heart talks with my pastor.

You don't make friends in the drug realm, not real friends. You can't. You don't want to, because if you become friends with someone who is selling a lot of drugs for you, and they start asking you for money all the time, what are you going to do? You don't make friends. You have acquaintances who do things for you, but you don't become close. There is always a wall there, always a barrier that keeps you from getting too close.

It's a lonely life, very lonely. And you have everything you could want, materially speaking. Money everywhere, but it doesn't bring you happiness. People all around who you think are your friends, but you can't be honest with them.

When I left that life, I didn't expect to see any of those people again.

But two of my friends kept coming around. One of them was named Donnie. We were really close for the three years leading up to my conversion, through the worst years of my drugs and drinking. He even drove a tow truck for me at one of my salvage yards, and we talked almost every day. Even after I lost the towing contract with the police, Donnie still ran some jobs for me, picking up the wrecked trucks I bought and bringing them to the salvage yard.

But when I couldn't give him consistent work, he started driving for someone else, hauling mail from Harrisburg to New Jersey every night. He rented a house that ended up getting sold, so he bought a nice camper and parked it beside a mutual friend of ours. So that's where he lived, in this camper.

He was a really nice guy, Donnie. Someone I could have honest talks with. And although he didn't give up his drinking, we had a lot of good talks about God. He was one of those guys who was a good listener and asked a lot of questions.

In the spring of 2016, the guy who owned the house where Donnie parked his camper realized Donnie's car was still in the driveway, even though he usually left for work around 5:30 in the evening. So he wandered over and knocked. No one answered, so he nudged open the door and shouted. Still no answer.

He peeked through the door. Donnie was lying on the floor, dead.

He had done a lot of crystal meth through the years, well before I knew him and we started partying together. I guess his body just fell apart. Couldn't take it. There were times when I was with him, all of us guys sitting around and drinking and he'd turn blue. Just like that. His head would drift backwards and we all thought he'd died, but then he'd jump up. He'd go to the doctor and the doctor would tell him, "You have to quit drinking. You have to quit smoking." There were so many times we thought he had died.

But when he was gone, it hit me again. God's grace for me. Because that should have been me, dead, for any number of reasons. That could have been me. There are so many people I knew back then who aren't alive anymore. Folks who died violent deaths or overdosed or had heart attacks at an early age.

But for some reason, God reached down and

found me, directed me to go to that church on Sunday morning, took away the desire for drugs.

I can't explain it. Why me and not Donnie. I don't know. But here I am, and I thank God all the time that he spared my life.

When I came back from the Dominican Republic for the first time, I started going to Camden, NJ. There was a ministry down there that I got involved in, and I started doing more and more work down there. I went along with a group during my first year of being clean, and I was attracted to Camden after that. I started going down there a lot on my own, or with two or three other people.

Why Camden? There are so many hurting people there. You really have to walk the streets in order to experience it, in order to understand it. Wherever you go, you see signs of addiction and poverty. It's a devastated city, but even in the midst of that mess, there are a lot of positive things happening.

So I keep going back. Sometimes I do small tent crusades there in the city, in the same areas. During one of our recent trips we parked our bus on Liberty Street, and it faced down the block towards a big, abandoned building on a quiet street. There's not a lot of traffic there because the area is so depressed – very few jobs in that part of the city, with lots of abandoned houses and warehouses.

I sat there and stared at that abandoned building. It was maybe eight stories tall, all the windows knocked out. Doors hanging off the hinges. But there was a steady flow of people in and out all day long, in and out, in and out. Drug addicts. I asked a few guys what went on in that building, and they said there's a guy in there who sells needles and syringes, and there's a guy selling heroin, and there are rooms you can go in to get high. It's basically a drug hotel for addicts.

There were police driving all around the block, but I knew after three minutes what was going on in there. Yet, the law doesn't do anything. The pastor of the church later told me that the problem is the jails are already full, so they don't know what to do with the people they arrest. There's no place to take them. And the people in the building don't care if they get caught because it's better for them in the jail than it is outside of it. At least in prison they have a bed to sleep on and food to eat.

I sat there watching, and there were girls, young girls, coming in and out. They were homeless, living under this bridge or that bridge, wasting their lives away. It's so sad. Where are the people who will help them? Where have all the Christians gone?

One time I walked the streets in Camden with a few students from the drug and alcohol rehabilitation center, Teen Challenge. We were evangelizing and praying with people. As we continued down a mostly empty street, we noticed three guys sitting in lawn chairs at the side of the house. We got closer. We didn't say a word. I might have looked over at them and nodded a hello.

One of the guys jumped up and stared at us before reaching up and pointing one of his fingers in my face.

"Listen," he said in a stern voice, "I know who you are and I know what you're all about. You need to get off my street."

"What are you talking about?" I asked. The three of us stopped and faced the three of them. The guy who was talking didn't lower his hand. He just kept pointing.

"You guys are Christians, and I don't want you here. I serve the devil. Look! I've got 666 tattooed right here on my arm." He pulled his sleeve back and showed me the tattoo.

"I want you out of here," he demanded. "There's a war going on between you and us."

"Really?" I asked. "Who's winning?"

"I don't want to talk about it," he growled. "Leave."

I shrugged my shoulders, and we kept walking, but today I would have handled that situation a little differently. I would have stayed and talked to him longer. Now, I have a better understanding of the power we have in Jesus.

Those were my early days in Camden.

I got to know the guys on the street there in Camden, and they wanted help but didn't have anywhere to go. There just weren't enough beds at the rehab houses in the area, and the hospitals wouldn't take them in anymore.

So I started bringing guys home with me. I didn't know what else to do. I was there telling them about the love of Christ – how could I walk away and leave them on the street? I lived in a garage in Bethel at the time, where I had my dealership. It was a two-bay car garage, and in there I had my office and a full bath with a shower.

In one of the bays we made a makeshift kitchen, and before I knew it we had set up two bunk beds and I had four guys living with me in this garage. Eventually I rented a house in Mount Zion and had seven guys. I had bought a bus at one point, so once I had too many guys at the Mount Zion house, I started sleeping out in the bus. I basically lived there.

I didn't have a lot of grand goals in mind. I basically wanted to disciple these guys, to help them see a better way, and to lead them closer to God.

I've met all kinds of guys during the last few years of doing this. There was an older homeless man named Jackson who played the guitar. He had been an alcoholic but quit drinking before he came to live with us.

Another guy had graduated from Teen Challenge, had even been on staff there and gotten back together with his wife, but somehow ended up in Florida doing drugs again. He called me from a church in Florida, and I helped him get into a rehab in Indiana. He could make one phone call a week there, and he always called me, of all people. When they turned him loose, I bought him a bus ticket and he came and moved in with us.

Another guy, Dominic, was on the streets in Camden and went to a detox center in NJ. That's where I picked him up.

We've had some success stories, guys who are working jobs and doing good. And of course we have guys who have gone back to their old ways. My intention has always been simply to give these guys a place to go to get away from their bad environments, give them a chance to rebuild their life, and help them learn how to focus on God. Really get God in their lives.

Running this home has had a tremendous effect on me. It's helped me to grow in the Lord. You know, I never went through a rehabilitation program myself, so doing this work with the guys, leading them through the Bible, helping them think about their lives, it's all been really good for me. I think, in some ways, it's helped me stay clean. After all, I know I've got all these guys depending on me, looking up to me. If I fail, a lot of them might fail, too. They've become my family.

My vision is to keep the home going, although I don't see it becoming some kind of a big rehab program like Teen Challenge. I want to keep it small, eight to ten guys. Manageable, with a number of guys that I can faithfully disciple and live alongside. I'm working on fixing up the third floor of the house we're currently in, so once that's completed we can probably have up to 11 guys there. That's my plan. I just want to keep it small and keep it going.

We use the home as a mission house, too, and we reach a lot of people in the city of Lebanon. Nearly every day someone stops by looking for some help, and we do what we can. We also do a morning devotional, and a handful of people come in each day to join us for that. I want this home to be a light in the city, a place where people encounter the love of Jesus and find freedom.

I also love to travel, and I want to keep doing prison ministry. You know, at first I didn't want anything to do with prison ministry, for a few different reasons. Mostly, I had been trying to avoid prison for decades – why would I go inside voluntarily? But also it seemed like so many people were already doing it. I wondered if there was even a need for more teams, more people.

But I realized after two years or so of working in prisons, that those things don't matter. I'm effective in prisons because of my story. Prisoners relate with me and what I've been through. They'll listen to someone who used to be into the same kinds of things they are into. They pay attention when someone is up front telling them a different version of their own story.

I also love doing street ministry in different cities, just walking around and letting the Spirit introduce us to new people, people who need to hear the Gospel. And I want to expand our work in Costa Rica. In August of 2016, I took my first team of 15 people down there. I know the pastors of a few churches, and they have started using the house I own there as a retreat center, so when I took my group down there we had services at some of those churches and reached out to the local communities.

My vision would be to get to the place where I am taking a team down there every other month or so, and I have a lot of churches that are interested. I just need to get everything in place so that we're not only making a difference for the people in Costa Rica but also doing the trips in a way that has a major impact on those going down and serving. I want to get something good started down there. Besides, Costa Rica is close to Nicaragua, the second poorest country in the western hemisphere, so maybe someday we can even branch off and do work there.

After my first trip to Costa Rica, I felt drawn there. Eventually, I closed my businesses and bought my friend's house down there. I have a Costa Rican couple who live there now and are the caretakers. There's a garden out back. He painted the roof and built 20 bunks. I even have someone who donated the mattresses and we shipped them down.

Well, I made me a home in San Carlos
Down by the Arinol volcano
And I grew me a Garden of Eden
Where I go walking hand in hand with Jesus.

He said, Son, let me share with you the meaning.
Don't waste your time like all the people
That go around dreamin' to live.
Go on and live your dream.

I took my first group down there in the summer of 2016, and we were there for about 2 ½ weeks. They loved the bunk house – it's not the Taj Mahal, but it's clean and comfortable. It's located in the jungle, and it tends to be a little on the warm side, but if you keep the air moving, it's bearable. In the afternoon, a few clouds will blow over and it will rain for a bit, which is lovely.

The people who came with me shared their testimonies and learned some Spanish songs. We went to different churches and did services there. During the day, we went into the city, visited an orphanage, and spent some time at a drug rehabilitation center. One day we even went on a jungle hike.

On a night when we didn't have a church service scheduled, I took them to these thermal waters at the base of a volcano mountain. The thermal waters are right there in the heart of the jungle, and they enter the stream among the river rocks. At that particular spot, the water gets hotter the further upstream you go, to the point where the water will almost burn you. We each found a hot spot and sat with our back against the rocks, the warm water running over our shoulders. As it gets darker and the air cools off, it's a beautiful thing. I think about that place a lot, but especially on cool evenings here in PA.

The service at the drug rehab was pretty incredible. There are 16 guys there, and the day after we were there the director called me and wanted to meet. He has a counseling center where he works with alcoholics. We met for an hour and a half, and he wants me to get more involved with his guys when I'm down there, to show up somewhat regularly and encourage them in their journey.

Those trips are busy times for me. I go over early and reconfirm with the churches. I finish up a few things around the house – this time I replaced a vanity and did a few other odd jobs. I am always burned out after everyone leaves, and that's a nice time to rejuvenate, in the quiet of the jungle.

I continue to stay in touch with the prisons down there. In fact, we had planned on going to one during this last trip, but at the last minute they canceled on us. I have a feeling it was because I had six guys going along with me, and they're a little suspicious of six Americans wanting to go into the prison. But I still feel a pull to minister to the men in prison down there. I've recently been in touch with another guy down there who goes into prisons on a regular basis, and he assured me that he can help me get in.

We call the house in Costa Rica the "Costa Rica House of Prayer." The community meets there twice a week for prayer and worship. I told the house parents and leaders I don't want it to be a church or anything that's linked with a denomination. I just want it to remain a house of prayer, where people come to find freedom in Christ and are released from the bondage and strongholds that keep them bound in darkness.

I had a lot of things in my life that left me wanting more. I was always searching for something. At 42 years old, I finally found what I was searching for all those years: a true relationship with Jesus Christ. In Matthew 5:6, it says, "Blessed are those who hunger and thirst after righteousness, for they shall be satisfied." I found the satisfaction I was searching for in a true relationship with Jesus Christ.

God healed me from a lot of things in my past. He healed me. It would be easy for me to look back over my life and find people to blame for why I did what I did, but in the end, it was my own bad choices and mistakes. I can't hold that stuff against other people. God healed me of all of it.

I have such a close relationship with the Lord,

and I can only be where I am today by continuing to walk in the Spirit. Jesus delivered me and set me free. All the strongholds and bondage, Jesus took care of IT.

Do I ever get tempted to do drugs again? Yeah, I do. You know, a person who comes from a bad drug or alcohol addiction, there are certain things that trigger us to want to go back. One of the main things is if someone lets me down or someone who I thought was my friend turns their back on me. That's the first thing that comes to my mind in those kinds of situations: I should just go get high.

The worst thing you can do with an ex-drug addict is bring them down or make them feel alone. You need to lift them up, stay positive. I can't be around negativity. The enemy tempts me, but God is there to take away the desire.

Maybe you're an alcoholic, or someone who's struggling with drugs. I want to talk to you for a second.

Look, my life was in deep despair. I tried so many times to change my life on my own, over and over again, but I just never got anywhere with it. I pulled and tugged and fought to quit. I couldn't do it. I just couldn't do it. Well, let me clarify that – I could do it for a week, or a month, but I always kept going back. Something had ahold of me that I couldn't cut loose from, not on my own.

It all changed when I submitted my life to Jesus. He's the one that changed my life and set me free from my addictions. An addiction is a stronghold, and the Bible says in 2 Corinthians 10:4, "The weapons of our warfare are not of our flesh but divine powers to destroy strongholds." The devil uses strongholds to control our lives, and addiction is one of them.

Addictions — we all struggle with them at some point. Maybe not alcohol. Maybe not drugs. But there are a lot of addictions out there. Religion without a relationship with Jesus can even be an addiction, one that the devil can use against us.

The only way to break the stronghold is with the blood of Jesus and the power of the Holy Spirit coming into someone's life and changing it. That's it. That's what sets someone free from addiction.

In Romans 8:2, Paul talks about being set free in Christ and if you keep saying you've accepted Christ but you keep falling back into your old life, you've not been set free. If you say you believe in Christ, but you keep falling back into drugs and then cleaning up and then falling back and then cleaning up again, there's still a stronghold there. If you've been set free, you are free indeed! You won't go back.

Do you want to be free? This is how you find freedom in Christ:

You get into the presence of God. You must believe in faith that Jesus is God's Son and you need him as your Savior. You ask him into your heart. You ask for forgiveness for your past sins. You renounce Satan and the ways of the world. You make a binding covenant with God. You commit to following Jesus. But that's just the beginning. There's a world of difference between the work Christ did in us and the work the Holy Spirit does for us. In other words, Christ is the one who sets us free and is our salvation, but we have to walk with the Holy Spirit if we don't want to return to that life of bondage.

Romans 8:14 – 17 says, "All who are led by the spirit of God are sons of God." When you receive the spirit of adoption as sons of God, you are now adopted into His kingdom. God is on His throne in His Kingdom. Jesus is on His right side. We, as adopted sons are now part of His kingdom, even here on Earth. We were born from the seed of Adam, with his sin nature. Now, as adopted sons, we are no longer of Adam's bloodline but of Jesus' bloodline. Addiction, alcoholism, the sin nature, does not flow in this bloodline. It is impossible for sin to flow in this bloodline. That is why Jesus knew no sin! He could not sin, because he was not of the seed of Adam.

It's so important that we recognize our new

identification in Christ Jesus. You are no longer identified with the old man in Adam. He died and is no more!

The world says, "Once an addict, always an addict."

The world says, "Once a junkie, always a junkie."

The world says, "Once in recovery, always in recovery."

But the Bible says in 2 Corinthians 5:17 that "if anyone is in Christ, he is a new creation. The old has passed away! Behold, all things are new!"

When the Bible says, "All things," it means "All things," including your new identification in Christ. Do not allow people from your past, including family members or friends, to give you your identity, because many times they still identify you as Adam.

When Jesus asks Peter in Matthew 16:15, "Who do you say I am?" Peter replies, "You are the Christ, the son of the living God." Jesus then said to him, "Flesh and blood could not have revealed this to you, but only my Father who is in heaven." Do not allow flesh and blood to give you your identification. Only your Father in heaven can reveal this to you.

Does this mean you won't be tempted? No! Paul says in Galatians 5:16 that if we walk with the Spirit we will not fulfill the desires of the flesh. He doesn't say anything about not being tempted by the desires of the flesh. They're still going to hound us. But if we walk in the Spirit, we won't act on those desires.

Christ is the one who set me free. Walking with the Spirit keeps me free.

One of the main ways the Spirit will lead you when you become clean is away from the people who keep you in bondage. You can't continue to associate with people in that kind of a life because they will drag you right back into it. Sometimes this means you have to completely change your environment. It might even mean moving to a different city or state, getting away from the environment where you know where all the drugs can be found. You can move into the middle of the Sahara Desert, and if you really want heroin, you'll find it. If you're not set free in Christ and walking with the Spirit, relocating somewhere else isn't going to do a hill of beans of good for you. Because you're still going to have that desire. You can find drugs wherever you go, because they're everywhere.

But change your friends. Change your environment. These things will help you stay clean.

Another big thing, is becoming part of a

fellowship. You simply must surround yourself with good Christian fellowship. Churches aren't going to save or deliver us, but they can help us grow. Churches will help you make new, Godly friends. Churches can help you enter the presence of God through worship and learn more about God's ways. It won't save you, but it will help.

Maybe your addiction is really bad. Maybe you don't have a Christian background. If you don't have any kind of foundation of knowing the Bible or walking with God, it's so important to get into a discipleship program. An extended program – not something for 30 days, but something that you have to commit to. A lot of guys hear me say this and their reply is that they have a job, they have to work, but my response is always this.

"What's one year? One year in your life? If that's what it takes to get you right, to get free from your addiction, isn't it worth it? What is one year compared to eternity?"

Discipleship programs can be very important.

There were times I wish I would have gone through a program, especially during the first year. I think I could have learned so much in that year about the Lord. I could really have benefitted from dedicated time to study the Bible.

But in some ways, I created my own

discipleship program – I stayed very involved in my church and men's Bible Study groups, and I studied a lot on my own. I didn't think I knew it all, and I still don't, but I continuously put myself in a place where I can learn.

And I don't know what I would have done without my mentor, Ted Williams. He walked with me and mentored me and still does. I would have considered going through a program if I didn't already have all of those things in place.

That's what I really want people to walk away with. God gets all the honor and glory for where I am today. There was a time in my life when all I cared about was my next drink, my next high. All I wanted was more toys. I had a nice house in Eagle Rock, a brand-new pick-up, a nice sports car. It was all about the image. All about the stuff.

I wanted to impress people.

Today, I don't care about all that stuff. I live in a small place, happy to have a roof over my head and a warm place to sleep. The things of this world don't mean anything to me anymore! It's all about eternity. I can't wait to go there. This world doesn't mean anything.

I see people, especially Christians, with all of

their nice things and beautiful houses and toys sitting around. What are they going to do with them? On the streets, every day, there are people dying and going to hell! How can we do it? How can we sit around with all of our nice things?

But I was there, too. I guess God let me go down that road. I had to. I guess other people have to go down their own road, too.

CHAPTER ELEVEN
THE SPIRIT WORLD IS REAL

One thing I've learned during these difficult years: the spirit world is real. You can't enter the battle for people's freedom from drugs and alcohol without coming face to face with it. You can't travel the globe, freeing those imprisoned, without seeing it. The spiritual world is very, very real. And we have nothing to be afraid of, because we serve the higher kingdom.

Within the last few years, I was in Lebanon, PA, in a coffee shop that I happened to own at the time. The coffee shop didn't last all that long, but the things I saw there impacted me like few other things in my life.

A young guy, maybe 17 or 18 years old, came walking in. He was small and skinny, and he wore a black hooded sweatshirt with the hood pulled up over his head. He came through the door and he was hunched over like he had a huge weight on him, and I could tell just by looking at him that he was lost. A lost soul.

I bought him a cup of coffee and asked him to sit down at the table with me. We started talking, just chatting about life, but something about him was so different than anyone else I'd ever spoken with. By that time, I was used to dealing with guys who were messed up on drugs or raging drunk. Trust me, I've seen it all when it comes to substance abuse. But this guy was different. The more we talked, the more I realized what it was: he was spiritual.

Everything he told me had a spiritual element to it, and I kept asking him questions to figure out where he was coming from. Finally, he started telling me about his dad, how his dad had worshiped Satan.

"When I was a baby," he said in a hollow voice, "my dad dedicated me to Satan."

He said these words straightforward, as if nothing was strange or odd about them.

"Really?" I asked. I had never heard that before in my life.

He nodded.

"Yeah. That's all I've ever known. I remember, when I was growing up, I'd go into the bathroom and see my dad cutting himself, sitting there covered in blood, performing blood sacrifices to Satan."

He went on to tell me horrible, horrible things, stories the likes of which I had never heard before. By the time he was 13, he sat in his bedroom burning candles, holding conversation with up to three demons that sat there in front of him. He was telling me all of this right there in my coffee shop, the first time I met him. It blew my mind.

But I didn't give him a hard time or jump all over him about the things he told me. I just sat there, and I listened. I let him talk. When he seemed to come to the end of his stories, I asked him a question.

"Do you realize there are two kingdoms?" I asked him. "There's a higher kingdom and a lower kingdom. There's a kingdom of light and a kingdom of darkness."

I paused and let that sink in.

"You're serving the lower kingdom. There's a higher kingdom out there."

"Yeah," he said, nodding. "I know. I know there is. I see a hand reaching down to me, sometimes, a hand that wants to lift me up. But I'll never be able to reach that hand, never be able to attain that kingdom."

"Why do you say that?" I asked.

"Because, when I was a kid, my Dad gave me

over to Satan. That's that. I'm in that kingdom and I'll never be able to leave."

I shook my head.

"No," I said. "That's the devil lying to you. You can switch kingdoms. Don't listen to that lie! I can help you switch kingdoms, but I'm not going to force you. I want you to do it when you're ready."

We talked for over two hours, and he filled me in on so many things about the spirit world, things I hadn't known before. This wasn't the first time I had dealt with someone possessed by a demon. One time, I drove a guy who was detoxing to a hospital, and on the way I asked him if he was ready to accept Jesus Christ into his life. He said he didn't know, so I asked him again. He said he didn't know. The third time I asked him that question, he answered differently.

"Yes, I am."

As soon as he said yes, this demon inside of him reared up. I was driving a Dodge Durango at the time, and he was in the passenger seat, and he arched his back as the demon roared out of him. It was a terrible sound. He twisted up like a pretzel right there on the seat, his legs bending backwards, up underneath him. I started rebuking the demon in Jesus name, and after a few minutes, it was out of him. Just like that, his feet went to the floor and his head drooped against the window and he passed out. That was that.

That was the first experience I ever had like that.

And now with this kid in my coffee shop. I knew he was in it deep. Real deep. It was the hardest thing in the world to watch him walk out of that coffee shop, knowing how deep he was in the occult. I didn't know if I'd see him again, and I so badly wanted him to experience freedom, but I wanted him to be ready.

I hadn't really moved from my spot, and ten minutes passed, when suddenly the door flew open and he came running in like a pack of wolves was after him.

"What's wrong?" I asked.

"I have to talk to you," he panted.

"What happened?"

"I was walking down the street," he said, looking over his shoulder, "and some guys were giving me a hard time, so I went over and I was going to cast a spell on them. But I didn't have any power."

He paused. I just kept listening.

"I lost all my power. I couldn't do anything. I felt weak and cold, and the only thing I could remember was the peace I felt when I was in here, talking to you. So I ran back here as fast as I could."

We stared at each other.

"I want that peace," he said quietly.

I took a deep breath.

"Are you ready to switch kingdoms now?"

"Yes," he said. "I am."

The words had no sooner left his mouth than the demon inside of him went wild. I've never experienced anything as crazy as that, but I managed to stay calm, rebuking it in the name of Jesus. This kid would fly at me to attack me, but when he got a foot or two away he bounced back as if he had hit a wall. He couldn't touch me.

There was an old man there with me. A quiet man who never said much. He'd just come into the coffee shop and sit there. The girl who worked the shop had gone out on the sidewalk, so it was just me, this kid, and the old man. This kid went on and on, acting wild for about fifteen minutes before slumping into a chair and passing out.

After five minutes or so I woke him up, and when he came out of that stupor, he was on cloud nine. He just kept shouting, "Jesus! Jesus! Jesus!" He was rejoicing and shouting, and it rubbed off on me. I went into such a spiritual high that night, higher than any drug had ever taken me. It was amazing.

The next day, that old man came back to the coffee shop.

"I gotta tell you something, Stan," he said.

"Ever since you've come into Lebanon, I've been watching you. There are a lot of false preachers that make their way through this town. I know. I've watched them, too."

He paused.

"But after last night, after seeing what I saw with that boy, well, I know you're the real deal."

I gave him a wry smile.

"Is that so?"

He nodded.

This kid and me, we've been on a journey together. A long journey. But he's experienced victory and freedom.

I wish every confessing Christian could experience seeing these kinds of things. It makes believers out of unbelievers, really quick. It makes you realize the spirit world isn't just made-up Hollywood stuff – it's for real. It also helps you realize the importance of walking daily with God so that when the tempter comes, you will not be easily deceived.

The question isn't if he comes, but when he comes.

When I look back over my experiences, I see God used it to prepare me for the future. Since then, I have encountered many demonic manifestations and demonic oppressions on people. This is nothing to be afraid of – I stay calm and humble and take authority of them in Jesus' name. I tell them where to go, and they go. They don't have a choice in the matter.

I've seen people in real life, and on videos, trying to cast out demons, and they're screaming and yelling and holding the person down. This is completely unnecessary and senseless. All you have to do is remain calm and take authority of them in Jesus' name, and they leave.

I have one goal, and that is to honor God with humility in the work he has called me to do. Jesus said not to rejoice in this, that the spirits are subject to you, but rejoice that your names are written down in Heaven.

That is what I rejoice in.

CHAPTER TWELVE
FREEDOM

I spend more and more time in prisons these days, ministering to inmates. I've been all through Alabama with an organization called We Care. In North Carolina, I know the prison chaplain, so he takes me around, and I do services in different prisons in PA and NJ.

Usually we have about a half hour of music followed by an hour or so of testimonies, and a short sermon. I want to bring them hope, eternal hope for their future. I focus on seeing people get set free in Christ. I want to see bondages broken. Strongholds destroyed. It's incredible, some of the things I've seen, and some of the stories I've heard.

In Alabama, I came across a 35-year-old guy who was 16 when he murdered both of his parents. All through his childhood, they molested him, and when he got to be 16 years old, well, he just couldn't take it anymore, so he killed them both. At 16, he made a terrible choice, but it wasn't his fault, what happened to him up to that point. Now he's in there for life, and sometimes it doesn't seem fair. Sometimes the system seems broken. But there you have it. It is what it is. It's a cruel, ugly world.

The Holy Spirit shows up at these prison services, and that's when guys find freedom. They come up front and before you know it they're confessing their sins, confessing unforgiveness they had harbored for decades, walking away from lifelong addictions. They'll forgive people who they've held grudges against since childhood, and the freedom on their faces when they finally forgive is like nothing I've ever seen.

The addictions they find freedom from are all over the board – drugs, alcohol, and pornography. All kinds of different things. But what is important is that they don't just seek healing – they have to seek the Healer! Get into the Almighty's presence, and you will be healed.

One thing that's become a huge stronghold for some people is religion. Religion without relationship is worthless. You might want to throw the book at me when you read that, but it's true. People are addicted to religion, and it can become a huge stronghold in their lives, something that controls them and guides them even more than God. Anytime you allow something to control you more than God is controlling you, that's a form of witchcraft. Without a relationship to Jesus, religion will be another tool the devil uses to control your life. It's sad, but I see it all the time. When Jesus preached about repentance, He was always talking to the religious leaders.

When I go into prisons, knowing I was so close to that being me, seeing the guys and hearing their stories, it makes me so unbelievably thankful that God saved me from ever having to go in there. It gives me all the more drive to serve him and do what's right in His eyes, to do what He's called me to do. Because God spared me from going in there, spared me from living that life.

And then, when I see people in prison finding freedom, it gives me the drive to do it even more, to spend more time with them. The longer I do prison ministry, the more I realize there are a lot of people going into prisons and preaching nothing but religion! That's not what these guys need to hear! They need to hear about the freedom available to them through Jesus.

I see men physically in prison but spiritually set

free. I see people physically in the free world but spiritually, they're locked up.

I have a heart for both sides: the prisoner and the common citizen. I'll go wherever God wants me to go to help people find freedom in Christ Jesus. He gave it to me as an incredible gift, this freedom in Christ, and I want nothing more than to see others experience that freedom firsthand.